New Directions for Student Leadership

Susan R. Komives
EDITOR-IN-CHIEF

Kathy L. Guthrie
ASSOCIATE EDITOR

Developing Ethical Leaders

Arthur J. Schwartz

EDITOR

Number 146 • Summer 2015
Jossey-Bass
San Francisco

DEVELOPING ETHICAL LEADERS
Arthur J. Schwartz (ed.)
New Directions for Student Leadership, No. 146, Summer 2015

Susan R. Komives, Editor-in-Chief
Kathy L. Guthrie, Associate Editor

Microfilm copies of issues and articles are available in 16mm and 35mm, as well as microfiche in 105mm, through University Microfilms Inc., 300 North Zeeb Road, Ann Arbor, MI 48106-1346.

New Directions for Student Leadership is indexed in Academic Search Alumni Edition (EBSCO Publishing), Education Index/Abstracts (EBSCO Publishing), ERA: Educational Research Abstracts Online (T&F), ERIC: Educational Resources Information Center (CSC), MLA International Bibliography (MLA).

NEW DIRECTIONS FOR STUDENT LEADERSHIP (ISSN 2373-3349, electronic ISSN 2373-3357) is part of the Jossey-Bass Higher and Adult Education Series and is published quarterly by Wiley Subscription Services, Inc., A Wiley Company, at Jossey-Bass, One Montgomery Street, Suite 1200, San Francisco, CA 94104-4594. POSTMASTER: Send all address changes to New Directions for Student Leadership, Jossey-Bass, One Montgomery Street, Suite 1200, San Francisco, CA 94104-4594.

SUBSCRIPTIONS for print only: $89.00 for individuals in the U.S./Canada/Mexico; $113.00 international. For institutions, agencies, and libraries, $342.00 U.S.; $382.00 Canada/Mexico; $416.00 international. Electronic only: $89.00 for individuals all regions; $342.00 for institutions all regions. Print and electronic: $98.00 for individuals in the U.S., Canada, and Mexico; $122.00 for individuals for the rest of the world; $411.00 for institutions in the U.S.; $451.00 for institutions in Canada and Mexico; $485.00 for institutions for the rest of the world. Prices subject to change. Refer to the order form that appears at the back of most volumes of this journal.

EDITORIAL CORRESPONDENCE should be sent to the Associate Editor, Kathy L. Guthrie, at kguthrie@fsu.edu.

Cover design: Wiley
Cover Images: © Lava 4 images | Shutterstock

www.josseybass.com

Contents

EDITOR'S NOTES

For the past several years I've been teaching a course on ethical leadership. Perhaps unconventionally, I stridently avoid emphasizing or highlighting the reasons typically given for why a leader needs to be ethical; in other words, I don't rip from the headlines the ethical failures of American companies or the ethical lapses of our sports or entertainment figures. Sure, these examples are plentiful enough, but my approach is less comparison driven ("I don't want to be like that") and more aspiration driven ("What do I want to be like?"). I ask my students to critically examine their own ethical commitments and convictions. I invite them to critically assess why they don't always live up to their own ethical standards. These two practices lead to a final challenge: I ask the students to articulate the practices and habits they've developed (or want to develop) that will help them become the ethical leader they want to be.

Aligned with my classroom approach, there are two presuppositions underpinning each of the seven chapters in this volume. The first is the gnawing reality that we don't always act ethically. There are no ethical saints. Rare is the ethical Olympian. Most of us are ethical weekend warriors (we think we can turn the ethical switch on at any time), and some of us can only be described as ethical couch potatoes. This all adds up to the persistent "gap" between what we know is the ethically right thing to do and what action we end up taking. For reasons explained throughout this volume, too often we choose to be ethically blind, deaf, or silent.

Second, each chapter describes how we can help students become more ethically fit. We can intentionally exercise and tone our ethical muscle. Some of our student leaders can avoid falling down the ethical slippery slope by becoming more adept at listening for and appropriately responding to various ethical pressure words and phrases. Several chapters explain how we can train our student leaders to anticipate the different "red flag" situations they will likely find themselves in as leaders, and the ways in which educators can create opportunities for students to rehearse and practice how to effectively respond when they find themselves in these ethically sticky situations. Finally, some chapters emphasize how important it is for educators to encourage students to find a coach, friend, or mentor who can serve as an ethical sounding board. Swimmers and golfers have coaches and so should students who are committed to practicing ethical leadership. In

New Directions for Student Leadership, no. 146, Summer 2015 © 2015 Wiley Periodicals, Inc., A Wiley Company
Published online in Wiley Online Library (wileyonlinelibrary.com) • DOI: 10.1002/yd.20130

short, every student can become more ethically fit. All students can increase their ethical strength. Our challenge is to inspire students to recognize that it takes a commitment to build and hone their ethical muscle.

In Chapter 1, I describe the behaviors of the ethical leader (such as being fair, honest and trustworthy, caring for others, and listening to others). I argue that it is critical for student leaders to communicate to their followers the ethical standards that form their group. Moreover, the student ethical leader is responsible for holding others in the group accountable for those standards. I offer recommendations on the ways in which professionals can more intentionally integrate the ethical domain into their work with students, including how to gently prod the "ethical silent leader" to be less silent.

Patrick J. Sweeney and his colleagues offer in Chapter 2 a number of promises for enhancing the moral strength of our student leaders. At the core of their chapter is the notion that students need to take "ownership" of their ethical behavior. They argue that campuses, when promoting ethical behavior, should avoid an overly legalistic approach and instead strive to articulate and implement an honor or duty approach that invites and challenges students to pursue what is ethical and right rather than simply avoiding what is wrong or illegal.

Chapter 3 highlights one of the fastest growing approaches to developing ethical leaders: the curriculum Giving Voice to Values (GVV). Mary C. Gentile developed GVV out of her own experience as an educator at Harvard Business School. The curriculum reverses or "flips" how educators traditionally teach ethics and leadership. Giving Voice to Values case studies and scenarios are not about figuring out what is the right thing to do. Instead, the curriculum helps students find the most effective ways to speak their mind when they know what's right. In other words, the curriculum is designed for students to answer this question: "Once you know what is the right thing to do, how would you get it done?" The curriculum also provides students with the skills, examples, and tools to meet that challenge. The chapter also offers case studies of how Giving Voice to Values is being used beyond the classroom in places across the globe, including a program in India, a university in Ghana, and on the cricket field in Sri Lanka.

Although moral philosophers and cognitive scientists might enjoy debating the appropriate age to begin developing ethical leaders, educators have long recognized that student development, including ethical development, is a life-long process. Chapter 4 examines the commitment of parents and administrators of Ravenscroft, an independent school in North Carolina, to put into place a comprehensive program that aims at developing ethical citizens and leaders from pre-K to high school graduation (and beyond). Working with colleagues from the Center for Creative Leadership, the school has developed a framework that focuses on the spheres of leading self, leading with others, and changing the world. The chapter explains each of these three spheres in detail (especially the competencies within each sphere) as well as the three distinct but overlapping cycles of implementation (i.e., how the initiative is implemented at the lower, middle, and upper schools).

Nance Lucas has long been a major force in explaining the different practices essential to developing student leaders. In Chapter 5 she invites the reader to consider how the practice of mindfulness is essential to becoming an ethical leader. In nontechnical terms, Lucas explains what is meant by mindfulness and how mindfulness practices have been shown to have a positive impact on a number of leadership-related outcomes, including reducing stress and increasing attention. Throughout the chapter, she reinforces how critical it is for students to be in touch with (and regulate) their emotions as they navigate the challenges of being a leader.

Chapter 6 is written by Jon C. Dalton and it addresses one of the most neglected and underexamined areas of ethical leadership: how and what to learn from an ethical failure. This chapter identifies three primary reasons why college students sometimes experience an ethical failure. The chapter also discusses the ways in which ethical failure can be a powerful teacher. Dalton frames the beginning and end of his chapter by offering a personal example of an ethical failure that he experienced when he was in college. His vivid example reminds us of how difficult it sometimes is for a student leader to courageously stand up to tradition or convention.

The final chapter is written by Weichun Zhu and his colleagues. The authors examine different leadership models (and their respective scales) to help the reader more clearly understand the similarities and differences between these models, especially related to the ethical dimension of leadership. The models that the authors examine include transformational leadership, authentic leadership, servant leadership, spiritual leadership, virtues-based leadership, and ethical leadership. The chapter concludes with a call for more research to help educators learn more about the complexity and dynamics of ethics-related leadership.

I hope you enjoy the abundance and clarity of ideas imbedded in each chapter. Along with each author, please join me in warmly thanking Autumn Heisler. Autumn is a student at Widener University who provided editorial support for this volume as part of a professional writing practicum course. Her intelligence, editorial acumen, and positive energy do not begin to vivify her significant contributions to me and to each contributor.

Arthur J. Schwartz
Editor

ARTHUR J. SCHWARTZ *is a professor of education and the executive director of the Oskin Leadership Institute at Widener University. He was a senior scholar at the United States Air Force Academy and served 14 years as a senior executive with the John Templeton Foundation, including 6 years as its executive vice president. Since 1992, he has focused his research on adolescent moral development.* His articles have appeared in the Harvard Educational Review, Journal of Moral Education, and The Chronicle of Higher Education, *among others. He received his doctorate in moral education from Harvard University.*

NEW DIRECTIONS FOR STUDENT LEADERSHIP • DOI: 10.1002/yd

1

This chapter describes the behaviors of the ethical leader and explores the reasons why leaders do not always act ethically. The chapter also offers five recommendations to help educators integrate the practices of ethical leadership into their work with student leaders.

Inspiring and Equipping Students to Be Ethical Leaders

Arthur J. Schwartz

Rare is the student leader who has not had to make an ethical decision. Sometimes the situation will involve a close friend who has suddenly asked the student leader to look the other way. Other times the situation focuses squarely on the resolve and willpower of the student leader to do the right thing even if no one else is involved. Yet what do we know about how best to equip our student leaders to be ethical?

In recent years, there has been a verifiable explosion of attention given to the topic of ethical leadership. Scholars across many disciplines are beginning to conceptually map and empirically study the antecedents and outcomes of the ethical leader. Much has been discovered. Regrettably, and as I argue in the final section, most of what scholars have learned has yet to inform the thousands of educators who work with college or high school student leaders.

This chapter has five purposes. First, drawing on almost 2 decades of scholarship, I identify the core behaviors of the ethical leader. Second, I highlight what empirical data suggest are the benefits and positive outcomes associated with being an ethical leader. Third, I examine the multiplicity of reasons why leaders do not always act ethically. Fourth, I strive to answer the question: *What motivates or inspires someone to be an ethical leader?* Finally, I offer five recommendations to help college and high school educators integrate the practices of ethical leadership into their work with student leaders.

New Directions for Student Leadership, no. 146, Summer 2015 © 2015 Wiley Periodicals, Inc., A Wiley Company
Published online in Wiley Online Library (wileyonlinelibrary.com) • DOI: 10.1002/yd.20131

The Behaviors of the Ethical Leader

Based on nearly 2 decades of research, Linda Trevino and her colleagues have identified five core behaviors of the ethical leader (Brown & Trevino, 2006; Brown, Trevino, & Harrison, 2005; Trevino, Hartman, & Brown, 2000):

1. *Integrity*—the ethical leader is honest and trustworthy ("walks the talk").
2. *Fairness*—the ethical leader is transparent and does not play favorites.
3. *Communicates ethical standards*—the ethical leader finds ways to explain and promote the ethical standards of the group as well as holds others in the group accountable for their own ethical behavior.
4. *Care and concern for others*—the ethical leader treats everyone with respect and dignity (see also Resick, Hanges, Dickson, & Mitchelson, 2006).
5. *Shares power*—the ethical leader listens to everyone's ideas and offers members a real voice (see also De Hoogh & Den Hartog, 2008).

It is critical to underscore the importance of individual differences when it comes to these five dimensions of the ethical leader. For example, student leaders may show a tremendous level of care and concern for all the members in their organization, but they may lack the highest levels of reliability and trustworthiness, because they overcommit and overpromise. Other student leaders may be exceedingly fair and principled when it comes to decision making, but they may have difficulty sharing power and giving others in their group a real voice.

Most significantly, student leaders may have difficulty holding others in the group accountable for their own ethical behavior. For a variety of reasons, many of which are discussed later in this chapter, it may be far easier for student leaders to personally model honesty and fairness than for them to proactively and consistently communicate (and defend) the ethical standards of their team or organization.

The five behaviors of ethical leadership are easier to practice in the professional context. For example, leaders in businesses and nonprofits can make ethics an explicit part of their leadership style and agenda (Trevino, Weaver, & Reynolds, 2006). They can experiment with the most effective ways to communicate and reinforce how essential it is for everyone in the organization to be honest, fair, and respectful. Business and nonprofit leaders can develop and implement tangible initiatives to reward positive ethical behavior, sharing power, or consistently showing care and concern for others (such as linking promotions to these core behaviors of ethical leadership). Moreover, leaders in the professional world can demonstrate to followers their willingness to discipline individuals who have failed to follow or abide by the clear and explicit ethical standards of the organization. Each of these concrete practices and steps may be difficult for a student leader to implement or embody, even if they are in positions of responsibility (such as a sports captain or the president of a fraternity or sorority).

Along an ethical continuum, Trevino and Brown (2004) identified four types of leaders. Some leaders are simply *unethical*. These leaders practice none of the behaviors described previously. Other leaders are *hypocritical*; although they may talk a good game (ethically speaking), the words of these leaders serve only to mask their self-interest and narcissism. Probably the most common type is the *ethically silent leader*. These leaders are fiercely honest and principled; however, they find it difficult—if not impossible—to communicate or defend their ethical standards to others in the group or organization. Finally, there is the *ethical leader*, the individual who consistently practices all five of the positive behaviors.

The Benefits of Ethical Leadership

Over the past decade researchers have identified an impressive range of empirical outcomes associated with the behaviors and practices of ethical leaders. The bottom line is unmistakably clear: *the ethical leader is a more effective leader*. When leaders are honest, fair, principled, and trustworthy there are real and tangible benefits for their group, team, or organization. Consider the following benefits of becoming an ethical leader. Your team members will:

- trust more,
- be more committed and exert extra effort,
- be less cynical,
- exhibit less counterproductive behavior,
- be more willing to report problems, and
- bully less.

Much of the research on the benefits of ethical leadership is grounded in social learning theory (Bandura, 1986), which suggests that followers learn what to do (or not to do) by modeling the behaviors of those in positions of responsibility, authority, or leadership. In short, we learn what is ethical by listening to and observing others—whether it's our parents and siblings, peers and friends, teachers in our schools, or supervisors in an organizational setting. Social learning theory helps us to understand why it is so critical for ethical leaders, including student leaders on our college campuses, to model ethical behaviors and reinforce the ethical standards of their group, team, or organization.

Why Leaders Do Not Always Act Ethically

At one time or another, all of us have fallen down the "ethical slippery slope." No one is an ethical saint. Researchers have recently been investigating the reasons why we are not always ethical (Kish-Gephart, Harrison, & Trevino, 2010). In some cases, it is nothing more than having insufficient knowledge or a lack of awareness (e.g., I didn't know personal calls were not allowed). There are those times, of course, when our self-interest overpowers or trumps our ethical standards (e.g., I cheated on the test because I was afraid of failing). Research suggests, however, that peer pressure is the most significant reason why college students do not always act in an ethical manner (McCabe, Trevino, & Butterfield, 2001).

Historically, colleges and universities have sought to increase the ethical reasoning skills of students as a way to increase the students' ethical behavior (Kiss & Euben, 2010). Recent research, however, has shown that there is only a modest correlation between ethical reasoning and ethical behavior (Tenbrunsel & Smith-Crowe, 2008). The problem is not that we cannot make an ethical distinction; it is that we do not have the courage or inner strength to act on what we know is the right course of action (Gentile, 2010).

The research also suggests that context is critical to ethical decisions and actions. Not all ethical situations are created equal. Some situations may evoke a strong ethical response (e.g., I could never steal from a member of my family), whereas other situations will fail to elicit such a visceral reaction. In 1991, Thomas Jones examined the "moral intensity" we give (or do not give) to any ethical situation. Jones (1991) argues that we are all ethical mathematicians, adept at computing the "magnitude of consequences" of an ethical issue (e.g., stealing one dollar is not the same as stealing one hundred). He also emphasizes the importance of "social consensus," which is the extent to which we perceive the old idiom "everyone is doing it," whether it be corruption in the workplace or drinking under the legal age.

Bandura (1999) developed a theory of moral disengagement to explain why we may act in an unethical manner. He sought to understand the different reasons why we "deactivate" the cognitive or emotional processes that usually stop or inhibit us from acting unethically. Bandura (1999) posited that there are eight reasons or mechanisms that we may use to morally disengage. All eight have been widely discussed in the ethical leadership literature; two of these mechanisms are especially salient for student leaders.

First, Bandura (2002) suggests that we sometimes act unethically when there is a "displacement of responsibility." In this situation, members of a group will disengage from any ethical responsibility because they believe that the person in charge, perhaps a supervisor or an upper-class student, has told them that it is okay to engage in the behavior. Second, Bandura posits that we might engage in unethical behavior when there exists a "diffusion of responsibility" (p. 103). This type of moral disengagement occurs when no one in the group feels personally responsible for the group's collective behavior (e.g., a keg party that gets out of control).

Building on the groundbreaking work of Jones and Bandura, scholars have identified a number of additional situational variables that may influence our decision to engage in unethical behavior (e.g., Detert, Trevino, & Sweitzer, 2008; Hoyt, Price, & Poatsy, 2013; Stenmark & Mumford, 2011). Following is a listing of these situations and an example of how each of these situations might occur within a university setting:

Performance pressure (us versus them; winning at all costs)—imagine a college athletic team culture in which everyone is so committed to winning that the team leaders look the other way when a few teammates start using steroids to increase their strength.

Threats to self-efficacy (pressure to be successful)—engineering majors who cheat on a final exam because they are in danger of failing a required class.

Decision-making autonomy (nobody will find out)—a student spends club funds in an inappropriate manner because s/he is confident that nobody will ever find out.

Interpersonal conflict (who cares?)—a fraternity brother disregards the rules of his fraternity because the fraternity president is arrogant and a bully.

Bias (friends help friends)—a student leader bypasses an agreed-upon selection process to help a friend secure a coveted position in the organization.

Managing important relationships (wink-wink)—a residence advisor decides to look the other way when it comes to a minor house rule because she really likes and respects the student leader who had violated the rule.

In sum, researchers have identified a significant number of contextual levers that drive unethical behavior, both by single individuals and within groups and organizations (Kish-Gephart et al., 2010; Moore, Detert, Trevino, Baker, & Mayer, 2012; Trevino et al., 2006). Regrettably, there is far less research on why some individuals (but not others) resist the temptations to engage in unethical behaviors.

What Motivates and Inspires Someone to Become an Ethical Leader?

The short answer to this question is role models (Perry & Nixon, 2005). Whether it is our mother or father, favorite uncle or grandparent, older sibling, or favorite teacher, we know from the literature that our ethical behavior, especially during childhood and early adolescence, is linked to our cognitive and emotional need to be seen in a positive light by those we look up to and admire (Tangney & Dearing, 2004).

But during adolescence, scholars have long posited that the pull and tug of the ethical role model loosens (Lapsley, 2007). What emerges during late adolescence and early adulthood is a psychological concept known as the moral self. Augusto Blasi (1983, 1984, 2004) pioneered understanding of the moral self and the ways in which it motivates and fuels our ethical actions. More recently, and based on Blasi's initial conception, researchers have been modeling and testing the notion that ethical leaders have a strong and stable *moral identity* (Aquino & Reed, 2002; Aquino, Freeman, Reed, Lim, & Felps, 2009; Reynolds & Ceranic, 2007).

The idea that a person's moral identity has motivational power is built on three presuppositions. The first is that individuals with a strong and stable moral identity have *internalized* a set of ethical commitments and beliefs, such as a commitment to being honest, fair, or kind. These commitments are central and essential to their identity; thus, these individuals are motivated to live by (and model) their commitments (Hannah, Avolio, & May, 2011). Clearly, identity-conferring commitments extend beyond the ethical domain. For example, some individuals have a strong commitment to their family whereas others have a stable commitment to the practices of a particular religious faith or to the standards of their chosen profession, such as a medical doctor or a military officer.

The second presupposition is that individuals with a strong and stable moral identity have *a strong desire* to act in ways that affirm and reinforce their ethical commitments. They look for opportunities to walk their talk. They seek out opportunities to enact their moral identity as a way to show fidelity to their own standards of integrity and self-consistency (rather than acting in ways that simply maintain their reputation as an ethical person). Furthermore, these individuals have honed a heightened sense of ethical awareness, a built-in ethical antenna that enables them to recognize when a particular situation or context is ethically charged, even when others might not be so ethically sensitive (Reynolds, 2008; Shao, Aquino, & Freeman, 2008).

Third, individuals with a strong and stable moral identity produce the *willpower* to overcome the barriers and temptations that we face in our everyday lives. Although all of us are tempted to behave and act in ways that are not fully ethical, individuals with a strong and stable moral identity have developed the resolve and courage, often through practice and the cauldron of previous experience, to resist temptation and firmly act in ways consistent with their identity-conferring commitments (Hannah, Lester, & Vogelgesang, 2005).

Self-authorship is at the heart of the moral identity concept (Hardy & Carlo, 2005; Kegan & Lahey, 2009; Magolda, 1999). Ethical leaders act ethically because that is how they define themselves. They are not motivated to follow ethical standards because of some externally reinforced reason (such as the fear of getting caught or letting other people down); rather, they act ethically because that is the sort of people they authentically are and want to be (Hannah et al., 2005).

Ethical leaders do not simply follow the rules when an ethical situation arises. They are constantly and proactively looking for opportunities to develop personal projects that align with and express their ethical commitments. For example, I know of one student leader who decided to stop saying the word "try." He avoided telling his friends that he would "try" to get to their game or event, because he was concerned that if he did not show up he was deceiving his friends. Keeping his promises was important to this student, and he developed a personal project to always keep his promises and to avoid making a promise he thought he might not be able to keep. Indeed, there is growing body of research suggesting that ethical leaders have developed the capacity to (a) critically reflect on past ethical decisions, and (b) self-regulate their future behaviors based on that critical assessment (Jordan, Mullen, & Murnighan, 2011).

Over time, consistently acting in an ethical manner becomes a part of the leader's character (Hannah & Avolio, 2011). The leader's ethical commitments, combined with the desire and resolve to act in accordance with those commitments, become the source, standard and fuel of the leader's ethical behavior (see Chapter 2 in this volume). The most current research suggests that ethical leaders have honed a set of cognitive and affective resources, such as values, goals and behavioral scripts, that they "access and activate" when an ethical situation arises (Aquino et al., 2009; Lord & Hall, 2005). As an example, imagine this scenario: during a fraternity meeting a popular member suggests a new pledge activity. The ethical leader will quickly recognize the potential ethical implications of the activity and be able to "access and activate" the appropriate response (a "script") that results in the fraternity brothers openly discussing whether the activity is or is not an example of hazing. The "script" is often just a few words that enables the ethical leader to properly frame the issue (e.g., "Guys, we made a decision not to haze our new pledges, so before we go any further we need to talk about whether this activity is hazing or not").

Scholars and researchers are currently testing the moral identity model to explain and predict the motivations and behaviors of the ethical leader, especially in situations or contexts where other leaders, in response to similar pressures and influences, might fall down the slippery ethical slope (Mayer, Aquino, Greenbaum, & Kuenzi, 2012; Stenmark & Mumford, 2011). In sum, the growing evidence is compelling: a leader who has a strong moral identity—an identity central to his or her sense of self—will be more likely to act in ways consistent with his or her ethical commitments than leaders who do not have a strong moral identity. The real challenge, and one that has yet to be examined by scholars, is to understand why some leaders have developed a strong moral identity whereas other leaders have not.

Five Practical Recommendations

Many of the behaviors of ethical leadership are already embedded in various leadership models discussed and used on college campuses and some high school programs, including servant leadership (Greenleaf, 1977), the exemplary practices of leadership developed by Kouzes and Posner (2007), and the relational leadership model developed by Komives, Lucas, & McMahon (2013). The following five recommendations are offered as suggestive stepping stones for professionals seeking opportunities to more intentionally integrate the ethical domain into the support they currently provide to student leaders.

Recommendation 1: Use the Language of "Live Your Values".   It is folly to think that a traditional-age college freshman or sophomore has formed a strong and stable set of ethical commitments. Yet are we doing enough, as educators, to help our students identify what they stand for from an ethical perspective?

The idea of "living your values" often helps people understand the ways in which their values and beliefs dynamically shape who they are and the decisions they make (Thompson, 2009). Like the idea of a "moral compass," the notion of "live your values" orients us. It tells us the direction to take, especially if we are lost or disoriented.

The language of "live your values" is suggestive, because it is personal (compared to suggesting to students that they work on their moral identity). During their high school and college years, we can find ways to inspire and challenge our students to identify and live their values. In short, the language of "live your values" suggests that students can begin to "own" their ethical commitments rather than merely "borrow" the beliefs and values of their parents or religious tradition (for a review on the importance of "psychological ownership," see Pierce, Kostova, & Dirks, 2003).

Questions to ponder: What are you doing to help your student leaders to "live their values"? How are you integrating the language of beliefs and values into your leader development programs and expectations?

Recommendation 2: Do Not Underestimate the Power of Ethical Priming.   There is a growing body of research that focuses on the benefits of subconscious priming on ethical behavior (Welsh & Ordonez, 2014). The notion of subconscious priming is simple: we do not always respond to an ethical situation as if we were ethical accountants tallying the ethical bottom line. Sometimes we *reflexively* and *automatically* respond in an ethical manner without forethought. The emerging research suggests that we do so because our ethical beliefs and commitments are "triggered" through exposure to related stimuli. A classic example: a student reads a story about bravery and courage for a morning class and in the afternoon he or she immediately responds in a fair or honest way to an ethical situation, without consciously thinking about it.

In short, ethical reminders work! The research by Welsh and Ordonez (2014) is confirming what we already know from practice: subtle signals in a variety of contexts can make a difference, ranging from ethical symbols, posters and slogans to a variety of ethical rituals, stories and ceremonies.

Questions to ponder: Are you using subconscious priming on your campus? Have you explored the different ways that symbols, posters, slogans, rituals, stories, and ceremonies can serve as ethical cues?

Recommendation 3: Talk to Your Students About the Dark Side of Leadership.   In his book *Meeting the Ethical Challenges of Leadership*, Craig

Johnson (2001) applies Parker Palmer's language of shadow and light to help us better equip our students with the tools to be ethical. Johnson (2001) argues that leaders have a unique set of ethical challenges, and four of these are especially salient to the college student leader: *the challenges of power, privilege, deceit, and loyalty.*

No matter a person's age or the context in which he or she leads, all leaders struggle with the shadow of power and its corrosive effect. The literature is replete with examples of leaders who abuse their position because of their inability to recognize the shadow of privilege. The shadow of deceit concerns the various ways leaders violate the privacy of others, use information for personal benefit, or prevent members of the group from sharing information that others have a legitimate right to know. Perhaps most significantly, leaders engage in unethical behavior because of their (misplaced) loyalty. Clearly, the shadow of loyalty is a burden that confronts almost all student leaders.

Questions to ponder: Have you integrated the "shadow side" into your leadership programming? In what ways do you openly discuss with your student leaders the challenges of power, privilege, deceit and loyalty?

Recommendation 4: Help Researchers Crack the "Moral Identity" Code.   Current research suggests that the moral identity construct is critical to the behavior of the ethical leader. Yet scholars know so little about the building blocks of a moral identity. What role do parents play? Peers? Religion? Crucible experiences? Education? Role models?

The time is ripe for student affairs professionals to help crack the moral identity code. In ways large and small, they spend every day finding ways to develop and strengthen the moral identity of their students. College campuses, and especially the ethical challenges that student leaders face, offer a wonderful arena for scholars and researchers to learn more about the ways in which a moral identity forms and coheres.

Questions to ponder: As a student affairs professional, what have you learned that might be useful to moral identity researchers? Might there be opportunities for you to collaborate with scholars on your campus interested in ethical leadership and moral identity?

Recommendation 5: Gently Prod the "Ethical Silent Leader" to Be Less Silent.   This is the most challenging recommendation and perhaps the most critical. Recall that the ethically silent leader is a highly ethical person but one who is unable (or unwilling) to influence others in his or her group to be ethical. This likely describes many student leaders. We know from personal narratives that there exists a real cost to students who take a principled stand against the status quo. It is often far easier for a student leader to comply, stay silent, or simply go along when the group is engaged in unethical behavior—even if doing so compromises his or her values and commitments. Moreover, recent scholarship suggests that individuals who do the right thing are often resented by those in the group who don't (Monin, Sawyer, & Marquez, 2008). In sum, it is not easy to take the ethical high ground when it means that you are more or less telling your friends that they are on the low ground.

But ethical silence is a powerful form of communication, sending a powerful message. It is critical, therefore, for educators to find ways to equip their student leaders with the skills and confidence to explicitly communicate the ethical expectations of their group, team, or organization, as well as holding others (especially their friends) accountable for their ethical behavior. In short: leaders do not let their friends act unethically.

Questions to ponder: How do you help your student leaders find ways to explain and promote the ethical standards of their group or organization? What strategies have you used to help student leaders hold others in their group accountable for their own ethical behavior?

Conclusion

The study of ethical leadership is no longer in the theoretical wilderness. Hundreds of scholars and researchers are trying to understand this essential approach to leadership. If there is one area that scholars in the field all agree upon, it's that ethical leadership is not easy. Gray areas abound. There exists a band of acceptable dishonesty that we cannot just wish away (Ariely, 2012).

Yet we are also beginning to conceptually understand and empirically confirm that leaders who have a strong and stable moral identity are more ethical. Our core challenge as educators is to help our students recognize that they will need a moral compass to effectively navigate the myriad of challenges they will face as leaders.

References

Aquino, K., & Reed, A. (2002). The self-importance of moral identity. *Journal of Personality and Social Psychology, 83*, 1423–1440.

Aquino, K., Freeman, D., Reed, A., Lim, V. K. G., & Felps, W. (2009). Testing a social-cognitive model of moral behavior: The interactive influence of situations and moral identity centrality. *Journal of Personality and Social Psychology, 97*, 123–141.

Ariely, D. (2012). *The (honest) truth about dishonesty: How we lie to everyone—especially ourselves*. New York, NY: HarperCollins.

Bandura, A. (1986). *Social foundations of thought and action*. Englewood Cliffs, NJ: Prentice-Hall.

Bandura, A. (1999). Moral disengagement in the perpetration of inhumanities. *Personality and Social Psychology Review, 3*(3), 193–209.

Bandura, A. (2002). Selective moral disengagement in the exercise of moral agency. *Journal of Moral Education, 31*, 101–119.

Blasi, A. (1983). Moral cognition and moral action: A theoretical perspective. *Developmental Review, 3*, 178–210.

Blasi, A. (1984). Moral identity: Its role in moral functioning. In W. M. Kurtines & J. L. Gewirtz (Eds.), *Morality, moral behavior, and moral development* (pp. 128–139). New York, NY: Wiley.

Blasi, A. (2004). Moral functioning: Moral understanding and personality. In D. K. Lapsley & D. Narvaez (Eds.), *Moral development, self, and identity* (pp. 335–348). Mahwah, NJ: Erlbaum.

Brown, M., & Trevino, L. (2006). Ethical leadership: A review and future directions. *The Leadership Quarterly, 17*, 595–616.

Brown, M., Trevino, L., & Harrison, D. (2005). Ethical leadership: A social learning perspective for construct development and testing. *Organizational Behavior and Human Decision Processes, 97*, 117–134.

De Hoogh, A., & Den Hartog, D. (2008). Ethical and despotic leadership, relationships with leader's social responsibility, top management effectiveness and subordinates' optimism: A multi-method study. *The Leadership Quarterly, 19*, 297–311.

Detert, J., Trevino, L., & Sweitzer, V. (2008). Moral disengagement in ethical decision making: A study of antecedents and outcomes. *Journal of Applied Psychology, 93*, 374–391.

Gentile, M. (2010). *Giving voice to values: Speaking your mind when you know what's right.* New Haven, CT: Yale University Press.

Greenleaf, R. (1977). *Servant leadership.* New York, NY: Paulist Press.

Hannah, S., & Avolio, B. (2011). The locus of leader character. *The Leadership Quarterly, 22*, 979–983.

Hannah, S., Avolio, B., & May, D. (2011). Moral maturation and moral conation: A capacity approach to explaining moral thought and action. *Academy of Management Review, 36*, 663–685.

Hannah, S., Lester, P., & Vogelgesang, G. (2005). Moral leadership: Explicating the moral component of authentic leadership. In W. L. Gardner, B. J. Avolio, & F. O. Walumbwa (Eds.), *Authentic leadership and practice: Origins, effects, and development* (pp. 43–82). Amsterdam, The Netherlands: Elsevier.

Hardy, S., & Carlo, G. (2005). Identity as a source of moral motivation. *Human Development, 48*, 232–256.

Hoyt, C., Price, T., & Poatsy, L. (2013). The social role theory of unethical leadership. *The Leadership Quarterly, 24*, 712–723.

Johnson, C. (2001). *Meeting the ethical challenges of leadership: Casting light or shadow.* Thousand Oaks, CA: Sage Publications.

Jones, T. (1991). Ethical decision-making by individuals in organizations: An issue-contingent model. *Academy of Management Review, 16*, 366–395.

Jordan, J., Mullen, E., & Murnighan, J. K. (2011). Striving for the moral self: The effects of recalling past moral actions on future moral behavior. *Personality and Social Psychology Bulletin, 5*, 701–713.

Kegan, R., & Lahey, L. (2009). *Immunity to change: How to overcome it and unlock potential in yourself and your organization.* Boston, MA: Harvard University Press.

Kish-Gephart, J., Harrison, D., & Trevino, L. (2010). Bad apples, bad cases, and bad barrels: Meta-analytic evidence about the source of unethical decisions at work. *Journal of Applied Psychology, 95*, 1–31.

Kiss, E., & Euben, J. P. (2010). *Debating moral education: Rethinking the role of the modern university.* Durham, NC: Duke University Press.

Komives, S., Lucas, N., & McMahon, T. (2013). *Exploring leadership: For college students who want to make a difference.* San Francisco, CA: Jossey-Bass.

Kouzes J., & Posner, B. (2007). *The leadership challenge.* San Francisco, CA: Jossey-Bass.

Lapsley, D. (2007). Moral self-identity as the aim of education. In L. Nucci & D. Narvaez (Eds.), *Handbook of moral and character education* (pp. 30–52). Mahwah, NJ: Lawrence Erlbaum Associates.

Lord, R., & Hall, R. (2005). Identity, deep structure and the development of leadership skill. *The Leadership Quarterly, 16*, 591–615.

Magolda, M. (1999). *Creating contexts for learning and self-authorship.* Nashville, TN: Vanderbilt University Press.

Mayer, D., Aquino, K., Greenbaum, R., & Kuenzi, M. (2012). Who displays ethical leadership, and why does it matter? An examination of antecedents and consequences of ethical leadership. *Academy of Management Journal, 55,* 151–171.

McCabe, D., Trevino, L., & Butterfield, K. (2001). Cheating in academic institutions: A decade of research. *Ethics and Behavior, 11*(3), 219–232.

Monin, B., Sawyer, P., & Marquez, M. (2008). The rejection of moral rebels: Resenting those who do the right thing. *Journal of Personality and Social Psychology, 95*(1), 76–93.

Moore, C., Detert, J., Trevino, L., Baker, V., & Mayer, D. (2012). Why employees do bad things: Moral disengagement and unethical organizational behavior. *Personnel Psychology, 65,* 1–48.

Perry, G., & Nixon, C. (2005). The influence of role models on negotiation ethics of college students. *Journal of Business Ethics, 62,* 25–40.

Pierce, J., Kostova, T., & Dirks, K. (2003). The state of psychological ownership: Integrating and extending a century of research. *Review of General Psychology, 7,* 84–107.

Resick, C., Hanges, P., Dickson, M., & Mitchelson, J. (2006). A cross-cultural examination of the endorsement of ethical leadership. *Journal of Business Ethics, 63,* 345–359.

Reynolds, S. (2008). Moral attentiveness: Who pays attention to the moral aspects of life? *Journal of Applied Psychology, 93,* 1027–1041.

Reynolds, S., & Ceranic, T. (2007). The effects of moral judgment and moral identity on moral behavior: An empirical examination of the moral individual. *Journal of Applied Psychology, 92,* 1610–1624.

Shao, R., Aquino, K., & Freeman, D. (2008). Beyond moral reasoning: A review of moral identity research and its implications for business ethics. *Business Ethics Quarterly, 18,* 513–540.

Stenmark, C., & Mumford, M. (2011). Situational impacts on leader ethical decision-making. *The Leadership Quarterly, 22,* 942–955.

Tangney J., & Dearing, R. (2004). *Shame and guilt.* New York, NY: Guilford Press.

Tenbrunsel, A., & Smith-Crowe, K. (2008). Ethical decision making: Where we've been and where we're going. *The Academy of Management Annals, 2,* 545–607.

Thompson, L. (2009). *The moral compass: Leadership for a free world.* Charlotte, NC: Information Age Publishing.

Trevino, L., & Brown, M. (2004). Managing to be ethical: Debunking five business ethics myths. *Academy of Management Executive, 18*(2), 215–228.

Trevino, L., Hartman, L., & Brown, M. (2000). Moral person and moral manager: How executives develop a reputation for ethical leadership. *California Management Review, 42*(4), 128–142.

Trevino, L., Weaver, G., & Reynolds, S. (2006). Behavioral ethics in organizations: A review. *Journal of Management, 32*(6), 951–990.

Welsh, D., & Ordonez, L. (2014). Conscience without cognition: The effects of subconscious priming on ethical behavior. *Academy of Management Journal, 57,* 723–742.

ARTHUR J. SCHWARTZ *is a professor at Widener University and the executive director of the Oskin Leadership Institute.*

This chapter reviews the literature on the moral self and student development and highlights the best practices for enhancing students' moral strength.

2

Building Moral Strength: Bridging the Moral Judgment–Action Gap

Patrick J. Sweeney, Matthew W. Imboden, Sean T. Hannah

Arguments have strengthened in recent decades for colleges and universities to take a more holistic view of the student educational experience (ACPA, 1996; ACPA & NASPA, 2010). Envisioning students as developing whole persons and purposefully designing institutional programs and processes that account for that vision make possible some exciting outcomes for students and the societies they will influence (ACPA & NASPA, 2004). One intended outcome of such models is to graduate students who possess depth in conceptual knowledge, the ability to apply that knowledge in practice, and the strength of character to live and lead ethically (AAC&U, 2007). Studies of such efforts have helped to illustrate and affirm that "all institutions, by offering specific curricular and cocurricular opportunities for students, can contribute to the development of values and behaviors that represent character development in their students" (Astin & Antonio, 2004, p. 62). Professionals working in the student affairs domain, with their unique and authentic access to students, can accelerate students' strength of character regarding ethical action.

But how do you develop student leaders so they consistently *act* in an ethical manner? We emphasize *action* here for reasons that we will clarify. Before we delve into this question, we specify that we view every student as an emerging leader, someone who can be a source of positive influence on others whether in a formal leadership position or acting as an informal leader. Our approach to student development focuses on developing students' identity, knowledge, skills, abilities, and attributes so they can engage in ethical leadership. We believe that seeing every student as an emerging leader in development is a philosophy that has its place in any educational setting. Any student, for example, can engage in ethical leadership—by serving as a role model, by stepping up and enforcing

NEW DIRECTIONS FOR STUDENT LEADERSHIP, no. 146, Summer 2015 © 2015 Wiley Periodicals, Inc., A Wiley Company
Published online in Wiley Online Library (wileyonlinelibrary.com) • DOI: 10.1002/yd.20132

group standards, by speaking out in defense of someone being wronged, and by talking about the school's or team's values to inspire others.

One conventional approach institutions use to develop students' ethical leadership abilities is to focus on students' moral decision-making abilities—the cognitive component. Some institutions require ethical decision-making modules as part of their curricular and cocurricular programs. They may use case studies to draw out lessons learned regarding successes and failures in ethical decision making, feature speakers on the topic, and offer any number of similar programs. Are these traditional methods used to shape students' ethical decision making effective in producing graduates who live and lead ethically?

Research results from the area of moral decision making and behavior indicate that many people are capable of making good moral decisions; however, they have a hard time generating the necessary motivation to take moral *action* (Jennings, Mitchell, & Hannah, 2014). The literature suggests that moral cognition or judgment capacity explains perhaps 20% of the variance associated with actual moral action (Hannah & Avolio, 2010; Rest, Narvaez, Bebeau, & Thoma, 1999; Walker, 2004). This disconnection between individuals' moral judgments and their failure to take moral action is known as the "moral judgment–action gap" (Blasi, 1980; Walker, 2004). Leaders' moral actions are essential for earning followers' trust and their willingness to accept the leader's influence and be led (Mayer, Davis, & Schoorman, 1995; Sweeney, Thompson, & Blanton, 2009). This indicates that schools can make a significant impact by providing developmental programs and environments that spur student leaders to take the necessary ethical actions to implement their decisions, thereby enhancing their effectiveness as leaders and citizens.

In this chapter, we explore how development influences students' ethical decision making and action by reviewing key adult development theories. Next, we introduce the concepts of *moral self* and *moral strength*. Detailed discussion focuses on the components of moral strength and how they can be leveraged to motivate students to act on their moral judgments. Finally, we share practices for enhancing student leaders' moral strength and conclude with key takeaway points.

Adult Development Theories

Adult development theories have significantly influenced and guided student affairs professionals' efforts to develop student leaders for decades (Wagner, 2011). Many of these theories propose that people develop along predictable stages of cognitive complexity, and interactions with the surrounding environment play a significant role in fostering a person's cognitive moral development. As people move along the stages of development, their cognitive complexity qualitatively increases, which provides them with a greater ability to understand their experiences and gain greater autonomy in making moral judgments.

The creation of a *holding environment* within the university setting, in which students' current states of development are confirmed and higher states are inspired, is critical for development. Students can be exposed to higher stages of development and receive the support to engage in experiences that push their boundaries of understanding with the opportunity to retreat for reflection and reintegration (Wagner, 2011; Winnicott, 1960). Some of the dominant theories include Erickson's (1994) and Chickering's (1979) theories of psychosocial identity development, Kohlberg's (1976) and Gilligan's (1977) models of cognitive moral development, Perry's (1981) theory of intellectual and ethical development, and Kegan's (1982) orders of consciousness theory of cognitive development.

The dominant development theories infer that (a) people at different stages of development have diverse capabilities to notice, process, and make ethical decisions; (b) consistency of moral judgment and ethical action should increase as people gain greater psychological autonomy to self-author their own identity and values systems; and (c) people at different stages of development understand and make meaning of their experiences differently (Chickering, 1979; Kegan, 1982). Student development professionals should understand that in any situation in which an ethical issue arises, some people will not notice the issue, and those who do will process the issue differently and come to different ethical judgments. This variability in students' developmental stages suggests that student affairs professionals should understand human development theories; contribute to the creation of environments that accommodate various levels of awareness and agency; tailor programs, processes, and policies to students' developmental needs; and acquire a deeper understanding of how students develop morally. Regardless, capacities such as cognitive moral development may explain only 20% of whether a person will take ethical action or not (Rest et al., 1999).

The Moral Self

The gap between moral judgment and ethical action suggests that other factors influence ethical behavior. The main premise of this line of research, best associated with Blasi (1980, 2004), proposed that moral functioning is a characteristic of the person inasmuch as an individual has internalized moral values and created an identity as a moral person (Aquino & Reed, 2002). Powerful self-regulatory mechanisms come into play once a person views and defines themselves by moral values. These self-regulatory mechanisms include agency over one's moral actions, a high level of vigilance and focused attention on cues in the environment related to one's moral values, and a drive to maintain consistency between one's view of self and actions, which all serve to enhance the motivation to behave ethically (Bandura,

1991; Baumeister, Heatherton, & Tice, 1994; Blasi, 2004). Results from this research suggest that moral judgment coupled with moral identity and its associated self-regulatory mechanisms tend to enhance ethical action.

This perspective is likely familiar to many student affairs profession-als. Many historical theories employed by student affairs practitioners have been supplemented in recent years by theoretical viewpoints that account for the multiple, nonlinear, and intersecting developmental pathways that students are negotiating at any given time (Dill & Zambrana, 2009; Torres, Jones, & Renn, 2009). Student affairs practitioners can find new oppor-tunities to develop students if equipped with theoretical frameworks that more holistically account for both moral thought and action. We suggest that practitioners should focus on developing students' *moral self*.

Based on their review of the moral psychology and behavioral ethics literatures, Jennings et al. (2014) compile a categorization of the moral self that entails five primary construct categories divided into two "sides" (see Figure 2.1). The first side is called the "having" side, focusing on moral judgment disposition, self-conscious moral orientation, and moral centrality. Moral judgment disposition relates to a person's propensity to use one or various moral perspectives (e.g., utilitarian, virtue) when making

Figure 2.1.   The Moral Self

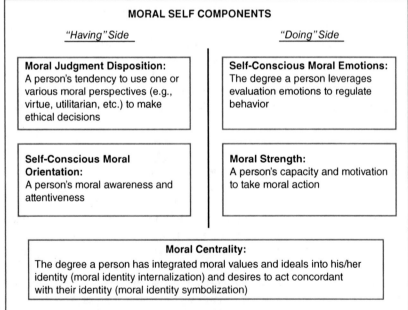

Source: Adapted from "The Moral Self: A Review and Integration of the Literature," by P. L. Jennings, M.S. Mitchell, & S.T. Hannah, 2014, *Journal of Organizational Behavior*, Copyright by Wiley & Sons.

ethical decisions. Self-conscious moral orientation entails one's likelihood to pay attention to moral aspects of their experiences and recognize and reflect on the moral implications of their actions. Moral centrality pertains to the degree that moral values and ideals are integrated into a person's identity.

In the model, the moral centrality construct influences both the "having" side and the "doing" side of the moral self. The "doing" side of the model focuses on three constructs that motivate one to enact their moral self in moral action: the symbolic aspects of moral centrality, self-conscious moral emotions, and moral strength. As noted previously, the symbolic aspects of moral centrality, or moral identity, raise motivation to maintain self-consistency and coherence by aligning behavior with one's internalized standards such as values and ideals. Self-conscious moral emotions reflect the degree that an individual evaluates his- or herself based on those internalized standards and uses the resulting emotions (e.g., shame or pride) to regulate ethical behavior. Moral strength entails the capacity and propensity to take moral action once a moral judgment has been made. Hannah, Avolio, and May (2011) describe this motivation or propensity to act on one's moral judgments as *moral conation*. Taken together, moral centrality, self-conscious moral emotions, and moral strength harness motivational forces to help a person take action to implement their moral decisions, assisting in closing the moral judgment-action gap (Blasi, 2004; Hannah & Avolio, 2010; Jennings et al., 2014).

Moral Strength: Conation

Moral strength/conation, that is volition or will, is a broad concept inclusive of many possible forces that may drive one to act on moral judgments (Hannah et al., 2011). Two elements of moral conation empirically tested are *moral potency* and *duty orientation*—two psychological states that research shows enhance an individual's moral strength to take ethical action (for overview see Jennings et al., 2014).

Moral Potency. This concept introduced by Hannah and Avolio (2010) entails three factors: (a) a person's sense of *moral ownership* over his/her moral behavior and environment, (b) beliefs in one's capabilities (*moral efficacy*) to act to achieve an intended moral outcome, and (c) the *moral courage* to act ethically in the face of risk or adversity. These three components are perceived as being state-like (that is, temporary or varying by situation), varying across contexts, and research shows they are influenced by contextual influences such as leadership and culture (Hannah et al., 2011; Schaubroeck et al., 2012). To increase the probability of moral action, educators should work to enhance all three components of moral potency (see Figure 2.2).

Moral ownership consists of individuals' degrees of psychological responsibility felt for their own ethical actions and those of others around

Figure 2.2.   The Components of Moral Strength

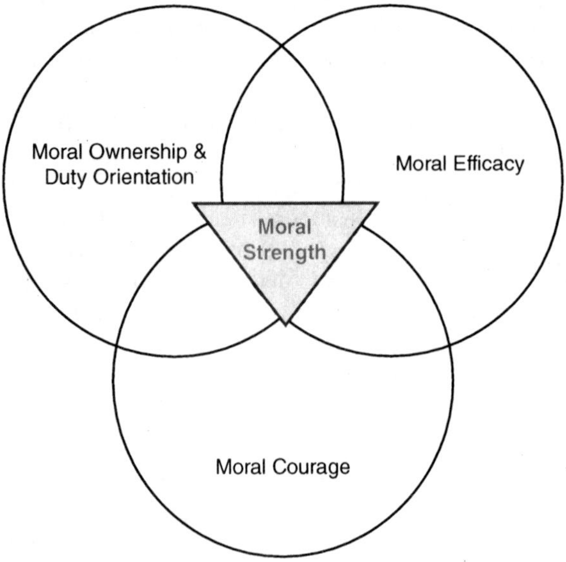

Source: Adapted from "Moral Potency: Building the Capacity for Character-Based Leadership," by S.T. Hannah, & B.J. Avolio, 2010, Consulting Psychology Journal: Practice and Research, 62(4). Copyright American Psychological Association.

them (Hannah & Avolio, 2010; Hannah et al., 2011). Felt responsibility is a critical factor of moral agency, a person's perceived capacity and orientation to exercise control over one's life, feelings, behavior, and context around them (Bandura, 1997). This assumption of responsibility for moral action enhances the motivational forces to self-regulate individuals to act in a manner consistent with those responsibilities (Bandura, 1991). Thus, agency forms the foundation for moral ownership, and the higher the level of moral ownership, the more likely a person will engage in ethical behavior (Bandura, 1997; Hannah & Avolio, 2010). Individuals with higher moral ownership are more likely to think "I (versus someone) should do something about this" after determining that something is unethical.

The second element of moral potency is moral efficacy, reflecting the degree of confidence one possesses to act ethically. According to this definition, moral efficacy is influenced by both a person's degree of self-confidence and an assessment of what external resources and means can be brought to bear to assist in the enactment of the ethical action (Hannah & Avolio, 2010). Research has shown that the extent that organizational leaders are seen as ethical and the organization's culture is ethical will positively influence the moral efficacy of individuals to act (Schaubroeck et al., 2012). If a student, who is captain of the soccer team, decides that confronting a classmate and teammate who cheated on an exam is the ethical thing to do, the student leader will not only assess his or her internal resources to confront the other student/teammate (e.g., interpersonal skills) but will also assess resources in the external environment that would support this action, such as the level of support expected from other teammates and coaches, and available reporting systems. This is known as means-efficacy. If the student believes he or she has the capability to enact the desired ethical behavior and external means would support this behavior, the motivation to act is enhanced (Hannah & Avolio, 2010).

Moral courage is the third element of moral potency, reflecting the fortitude to face risk and overcome fears (Kidder, 2003). Courage is viewed as being state-like in nature and varying between contexts, and in line with this conceptualization, research has shown that moral courage is influenced by organizational leadership (Hannah et al., 2013). It emerges in individuals as they interact with the environment and marshal the necessary psychological resources to meet and overcome perceived fear, risk, or social forces to take actions consistent with values and beliefs (Hannah, Sweeney, & Lester, 2007). Moral courage combined with feeling a responsibility to act ethically and a high sense of confidence that one can enact the desired ethical behavior provides the individual the moral strength to act ethically despite the challenges and perceived adverse consequences (Hannah & Avolio, 2010). Each of the elements of moral potency is thus theorized to be necessary but not sufficient.

Duty Orientation.   Another factor underpinning moral strength is individuals' levels of duty orientation, defined as "an individual's volitional orientation to loyally serve and faithfully support other members of the group, to strive and sacrifice to accomplish the tasks and missions of the group, and to honor its codes and principles" (Hannah, Jennings, Bluhm, Peng, & Schaubroeck, 2014, p. 220). Most traditional theories of morality are individualistic in approach, focusing on concepts such as postconventional reasoning or self-authorship, suggesting that the individual has transcended social conventions (Kegan, 1982). Yet individuals have critical responsibilities to others. To understand moral action, we must understand the motivations to fulfill those responsibilities (Folger, 2012; Folger, Ganegoda, Rice, Taylor, & Wo, 2013). If individuals have internalized their responsibilities to others, they are more likely to support those duties (Blasi, 2004; Sweeney & Fry, 2012). This internalized duty orientation creates self-regulatory mechanisms that motivate moral action in support of the group. Similarly, duty orientation bolsters moral potency by enhancing the moral ownership component. That is, if individuals have internalized a set of duties, they are more likely to take ownership and act when something is threatening those responsibilities. In a series of field studies, Hannah and colleagues (2014) found that ethical and transformational leadership were positively related to followers' levels of duty orientation, which in turn led to ethical behaviors. This suggests that duty orientation is malleable and contextually situated.

In summary, the adult development and moral-self literatures suggest that educational institutions should adjust cocurricular and extracurricular activities as well as policies, procedures, practices, and systems to foster the development of both students' moral strength and ethical decision-making skills.

Promising Practices for Enhancing Student Leaders' Moral Strength

The postsecondary environment has a longstanding association with moral development—and presents a variety of opportunities for developing the necessary antecedents for students' moral action (Pascarella & Terenzini, 2005). In an effort to foster moral action, it is important to consider some practical ways for faculty members and student affairs colleagues to focus their development of students' moral strength. The recommendations below provide some often over-lapping and mutually reinforcing starting points to consider. They range from institution-wide tactics that underscore the power of making such moral activity what Richard Morrill (1980) calls "the reigning values in the total conduct of campus life" (p. 116), down to more precise and discrete programming.

Enhancing Students' Moral Ownership

The institution's culture plays a significant role in creating a holding environment that encourages students to take responsibility both for their own ethical actions and for those of other members of the campus community. Educational institutions codify their cultures using vision, mission, values, and/or guiding principles statements (Schein, 2010). These ideologies should emphasize the importance of personal responsibility for ethical actions (Blasi, 2004). For example, Wake Forest University's School of Business holds an honor affirmation ceremony and honor training program as part of the new student orientation process that emphasizes both personal and shared peer responsibility for the code.

It is important, however, to guard against these expectations becoming nothing more than platitudes. First, students need to understand how each expectation should be enacted. How exactly is a student expected to act honorably? What acts are considered honorable and what acts are dishonorable? The former is critical as universities normally take a preventive approach by emphasizing what students should *not* do (e.g., lie, cheat, or steal) but rarely communicate the aspirational aspects of what students *should* do. The latter is of course more inspiring to students and can motivate development. Badaracco (1997) notes that things like values often fail to provide guidance when facing right versus right and wrong versus wrong situations. Universities thus need to articulate values hierarchies to students if students are to understand the priorities of their responsibilities and duties.

Furthermore, the institution's culture should communicate to students that they have certain duties in order to retain the privilege of being a member of the community. The intent is for students to freely embrace their obligations to support the community and develop a duty orientation toward those obligations (Hannah et al., 2014). To increase students' sense of duty and honor, it is important to understand that respect is the other side of the honor and duty "coin." People tend to honor and are dutiful to those things that they respect—thus actions need to be taken to raise students' respect for important principles and entities.

Recruitment and Admissions.   Processes institutions use to recruit and select students to join their communities are other mechanisms that can be leveraged to enhance moral ownership. Recruiters should clearly communicate the institution's mission, core values, and expectations of students and graduates with an emphasis on personal responsibility. The admissions application could include assessments regarding personal responsibility, such as having candidates respond to scenarios pertaining to personal responsibility for ethical action, asking candidates to share a personal experience that illustrates personal responsibility, or having recommenders assess candidates in these areas.

Role Modeling.   Role modeling by staff and faculty is another powerful means to bring to life a culture that values moral ownership (Schein, 2010). Students who see staff and faculty conducting themselves ethically on a daily basis will realize that their personal responsibility for ethical action is important to the institution's community. Furthermore, students learn ways to build moral ownership and its relevance through observing role models.

Honor System.   An honor system is also a powerful mechanism to encourage students to assume moral ownership and promote ethical action within the community (McCabe, Butterfield, & Trevino, 2012). A complete view of an honor system entails the code, education programs regarding the code and its enforcement, enforcement processes, and the development of an honor culture. Many institutions have developed honor codes that ask community members not to conduct acts such as lying, cheating, stealing or to tolerate those who do. These main tenets embrace both the individual aspect of moral ownership (i.e., not lie, cheat, or steal) and the collective obligation (i.e., not tolerate those that do). Students seem comfortable assuming the individual aspects of moral ownership regarding the honor code but struggle with assuming the collective aspect of moral ownership to ensure others comply with the code (Kegan, 1982; McCabe et al., 2012).

Orientation.   Senior university leaders should play a visible role in honor training programs, particularly during new student orientations. Such orientations should provide students an overview of the honor system; an understanding of how honorable behavior links to the institution's core values and mission; an appreciation for the relevance of honor to the individual, organization, community, and the institution's brand; a clear message that each individual is always responsible for ethical actions; an overview of what is honorable and dishonorable behavior and how to deal with values conflicts; and an opportunity to ask questions about the system. Having senior leaders play active roles alongside students during such sessions communicates to students that honorable behavior is important to the community and that each individual has a responsibility to behave honorably and ensure others do the same. To further enhance moral ownership during orientations some institutions incorporate various rites or traditions to mark the important transitional moment—including shared recitations, signing of names, interactions or rituals at significant or symbolic campus locations, and production of artifacts for public display.

Student Conduct.   Student conduct and judicial systems are key places where institutions can articulate moral values and expectations and are crucial arenas for encouraging and rewarding student moral ownership and action. In both academic integrity and general student conduct environments, universities should also consider whether theirs is a legal culture or an honor culture. In a legal culture, individuals are driven by rules and regulations and seek largely to avoid anything that would break such rules—a prevention focus. An honor culture is a promotion-focused orientation, wherein students are driven not to avoid wrong but pursue right. As noted previously, this starts with the very wording of the honor code, phrasing it in aspirational versus preventive terms. We recommend that when possible, any accompanying enforcement processes be grounded on an aspirational and developmental philosophy versus prevention and attrition philosophy. Anchoring enforcement processes on the foundation of moral ownership communicates to students that dishonorable behavior cannot be blamed on others or rationalized.

Recognition Programs.   Recognition programs are another mechanism educational leaders can leverage to enhance students' moral ownership. Awards focused on recognizing students who embody moral ownership or epitomize campus values are effective means to reinforce the importance of moral ownership and also increase the likelihood of similar ethical behavior throughout the community (McCabe et al., 2012). Thus, award programs both directly and indirectly reinforce moral ownership and ethical action throughout the community (Bandura, 1991).

Student Clubs and Organizations.   For student affairs professionals working with student organizations, there are tremendous opportunities for developing moral ownership in such settings rich with peer influence. For existing student groups, any transition moment where new organizational leaders are installed or new members are welcomed is an opportunity to allow the moral values of the group take center stage. Those expectations should be made very clear to prospective members during initiation.

NEW DIRECTIONS FOR STUDENT LEADERSHIP • DOI: 10.1002/yd

Member and leader nomination forms or operational handbooks can prioritize those concepts, and staff can design leadership transition document templates that encourage outgoing leaders to reflect on the importance of moral standards in the life of the organization for the benefit of future members. Educators in a position to craft or curate the processes by which new groups are chartered on their campuses can make documented moral expectations of group membership required elements of chartering or budget allocation processes.

Assessment.   Campus or division-wide assessment frameworks and student development goal statements are means that can be leveraged to enhance students' moral ownership. We encourage the use of individual student inventories and assessments to stimulate students' moral reflection. Feedback from self and others on assessments pertaining to personal responsibility and ethical behavior increases students' awareness on how others perceive them from a moral point of view. Any deficits in ratings might prompt students to further develop and enhance their commitment to personal responsibility for ethical action.

Enhancing Students' Moral Efficacy

Moral efficacy is a matter of students' skills and abilities for taking moral actions, including both their internal resources for meeting the challenge as well as the degree to which they identify external resources for support (Hannah & Avolio, 2010). Individual moral self-efficacy is an area where student affairs professionals can make a profound contribution by helping students to build skills for moral action.

Simulations and Role Play.   Highly realistic simulations and role play are excellent ways to build these skills. Resident adviser training programs including such simulated challenges for student leaders and can effectively help students enhance their moral efficacy. If fellow students are key contributors to framing the experience and offering constructive feedback to the student, the experience is strengthened even more. Similar approaches can be taken with other student leadership development programs. An example simulation may be related to the capacity to effectively address an observed unethical action with a peer who transgressed. Students can be trained in the interpersonal skills needed to have a constructive conversation with the individual, then practice those skills in a simulation to gain confidence. Moreover, appropriate scaffolding should be put in place (e.g., scenario scripts, assessments, after action reviews), to help students to limit the rationalization of moral inaction or the avoidance of moral issues.

Developmental Sequencing.   An important outcome is for students to see themselves as moral actors with the resources to claim and maintain that identity across various settings and circumstances. When designing such role-play programs, simulations can be developmentally sequenced and made progressively more difficult or complex, requiring students to build on previous learning and continue to push the boundaries of their comfort zones. To this end, the listening and dialogue skills for navigating interpersonal conflict and disagreement that many student affairs professionals help to teach on a regular basis are incredibly important.

Role Modeling.   The importance and power of successful role modeling on the part of student affairs professionals cannot be overstated here. Relationships with trusted student affairs staff are important places students can see and hear about moral efficacy in action. Authentic role modeling can enable students to learn about the situational nuances and associated personal struggles that moral actors experience and have their own experiences of those challenges affirmed (Hall & Davis, 1975). The developmental environment for moral efficacy is enriched when mentors can have conversations with students about identifying social pressures or other obstacles to moral action and then planning about how one might successfully plan moral actions that avoid the alienation of peers and other negative social consequences where possible.

Offering Support.   Student affairs professionals should also bolster students' perception of means efficacy regarding taking ethical action. Students need to be aware of and believe that external resources such as the honor code reporting processes, student affairs professionals, counselors, peers, organizational policies to prevent retaliation, and so on will support them when they take ethical action. If students believe that outside resources will support them, and they possess the skills necessary to enact ethical action, the combination bolsters moral efficacy, which increases their motivation to act honorably (Hannah & Avolio, 2010).

Enhancing Students' Moral Courage

Students exhibit moral courage when they act ethically or refrain from acting unethically in the face of risk (Hannah & Avolio, 2010). It takes courage to *not* act. "Not doing anything can be an act of cowardice, but saying 'no' can also be an act of real courage" (Putman, 2010, p. 15). One of the most significant things that practitioners can do to help bolster students' moral courage to navigate such risks is to create an environment that values and rewards ethical action (Hannah et al., 2007). This can be accomplished in a number of ways, such as visibly role-modeling ethical action.

Role Modeling.   Observing others acting with moral courage provides students with behavior scripts, ideas for support, and boosts their confidence to act similarly (Walker & Henning, 2004). Taking courageous stands in the face of risk or fear is difficult and can often be socially compromising for students. Student affairs professionals, student peers, and paraprofessionals need to be seen and heard cheering loudly for community members who act morally and also provide a morally affirming social presence to support moral action.

Reflection.   Moral courage can also be effectively enhanced when student affairs professionals enact frameworks to guide and successfully encourage reflection exercises on the part of students. When students are able to identify morally courageous actions and positively attribute them to their developing self-concept, they can bolster their ability to act similarly in the face of fear in future situations (Kihlstrom, Beer, & Klein, 2003). Values reflection exercises also assist students in clarifying their values and understanding the importance of possessing the courage to live by them. Moral perspective-taking exercises expose students to different ways to view moral action, which serves to broaden their perspectives, enhance their understanding of the factors that influence ethical behavior, increase their appreciation of the consequences of taking or not taking ethical action, and differentiating and integrating their values, contributing to the capacity for moral courage.

Practicing.   Finally, we again underscore the importance of giving students the opportunity to practice moral action by participating in simulations or considering case studies that place them in situations that call for the enactment of moral courage. Emerging evidence suggests that programs designed specifically to increase moral courage may be effective (Jonas, Boos, & Brandstätter, 2007). Such programs can teach people behavioral scripts (a sequence of steps) they can employ when moral courage is needed in the face of fear and risk, which helps students be more prepared to enact the planned behaviors and not be paralyzed by fear.

As with our discussion of moral efficacy, these skills for action require spaces and structure where students can practice living out these commitments. Moral courage can be gained through incrementally increasing the level of risk. Student affairs professionals can make these scenario-based experiences have more impact by providing assessment tools and frameworks that provide immediate and high-quality feedback to students. Scenario-based rubrics that provide developmentally rich descriptions of morally courageous thought and action are tools used by students, peer participants, and student affairs facilitators in such settings.

Key Takeaway Points

- *Set the example* (role modeling) is a powerful means student affairs professionals can use to enhance students' moral strength.
  - Set the example for moral behavior and ensure other team members do the same.

- Bring in character exemplars as guest speakers or include discussions of negative role models in programming.
- Ensure values, character, and ethical actions are considered in the staff and faculty hiring processes.
- *Engage students in dialogue* regarding their responsibilities of being part of an honorable community and the relevance of moral action to personal and organizational success and reputation.
  - Discuss ethical lapses that are part of current events.
  - Faculty and staff engage students in authentic dialogue about how they themselves have taken or have failed to take ethical action.
  - Talk about the importance of character and ethical action as a part of the alumni brand, a competitive advantage in the job market, and well-functioning societies.
- *Moral strength training programs* design to provide students with the interpersonal skills, scripts, and confidence to take ethical action.
  - Leverage simulations such as interactive role-playing and case studies to build skills and scripts.
  - Provide students opportunities to practice conflict management skills.
  - Create mentoring programs, such as peer-to-peer or with adult leaders of character, to engage students about values and the importance of ethical action for their developing identities.
- *Recognition programs* are influential means to enhance students' moral strength.
  - Applaud and affirm ethical behaviors that require students to take courageous stands.
- *Individual assessments* pertaining to moral strength, especially when paired with follow-up reflection and goal-setting, enhance students' moral action.
- An *honor system*, especially if it is aspirational, fosters the development of students' moral strength and contributes to ethical action.
  - Provide means for and publically signal student ownership of the code.
  - Conduct and judicial systems, especially when aspirational, can also be effective tools for fostering moral strength.
  - Account for the important distinctions between an honor vs. legal culture.
  - A developmental perspective regarding enforcement and sanctioning practices are key.
- The organization's deliberate integration of values and the expectation for honorable action into *cultural mechanisms* promote the development of students' moral strength.
  - Codify values, mission, and vision that include considerations of moral strength.
  - Define values in behavioral terms and provide values hierarchies.
  - Recruiting, admissions, and orientation processes can emphasize the importance of and communicate expectations of honorable behavior.

References

American College Personnel Association [ACPA]. (1996). *Student learning imperative: Implications for student affairs.* Washington, DC: Author.

American College Personnel Association & National Association of Student Personnel Administrators [ACPA & NASPA]. (2004). *Learning reconsidered: A campus-wide focus on the student experience.* Washington, DC: Authors.

American College Personnel Association & National Association of Student Personnel Administrators [ACPA & NASPA]. (2010). *Envisioning the future of student affairs: Final report of the task force on the future of student affairs: Appointed jointly by ACPA and NASPA.* Retrieved from: http://www.naspa.org/images/uploads/main/Task_Force _Student_Affairs_2010_Report.pdf

Aquino, K., & Reed, A. (2002). The self-importance of moral identity. *Journal of Personality and Social Psychology, 83,* 1423–1440.

Association of American Colleges and Universities [AAC&U]. (2007). *College learning for the new global century.* Washington, DC: Author.

Astin, H. S, & Antonio, A. L. (2004). The impact of college on character development. *New Directions for Institutional Research, 122,* 55–64.

Badaracco, J. L. (1997). *Defining moments: When managers must choose between right and right.* Boston, MA: Harvard Business School Press.

Bandura, A. (1991). Social cognitive theory of moral thought and action. In W. Kurtines & J. Gewirtz (Eds.), *Handbook of moral behavior and development* (pp. 45–103). Hillsdale, NJ: Lawrence Erlbaum Associates.

Bandura, A. (1997). *Self-efficacy: The exercise of control.* New York, NY: Freeman.

Baumeister, R., Heatherton, T. F., & Tice, D. M. (1994). *Losing control: How and why people fail at self-regulation.* San Diego, CA: Academic Press.

Blasi, A. (1980). Bridging moral cognition and moral action: A critical review of the literature. *Psychological Bulletin, 88,* 1–45.

Blasi, A. (2004). Moral functioning: Moral understanding and personality. In D. Lapsley & D. Narvaez (Eds.), *Moral development, self, and identity* (pp. 335–347). Mahwah, NJ: Lawrence Erlbaum Associates.

Chickering, A. R. (1979). *Education and identity.* San Francisco, CA: Jossey-Bass.

Dill, B. T., & Zambrana, R. E. (2009). *Emerging intersections: Race, class, and gender in theory, policy, and practice.* New Brunswick, NJ: Rutgers University Press.

Erickson, E. H. (1994). *Identity and the life cycle.* New York, NY: Norton.

Folger, R. (2012). Deonance: Behavioral ethics and moral obligation. In D. De Cremer & A. E. Tenbrunsel (Eds.), *Behavioral business ethics, shaping an emerging field* (pp. 121–139). New York, NY: Routledge.

Folger, R., Ganegoda, D., Rice, D., Taylor, R., & Wo, H. (2013). Bounded autonomy and behavioral ethics: Deonance and reactance as competing motives. *Human Relations, 66,* 905–924.

Gilligan, C. (1977). In a different voice: Women's conceptions of self and morality. *Harvard Educational Review, 47,* 481–517.

Hall, R. T., & Davis, J. U. (1975). *Moral education in theory and practice.* Buffalo, NY: Prometheus Books.

Hannah, S. T., & Avolio, B. J. (2010). Moral potency: Building the capacity for character-based leadership. *Consulting Psychology Journal: Practice and Research, 62(4),* 291–310.

Hannah, S. T., Avolio, B. J., & May, D. R. (2011). Moral maturation and moral conation: A capacity approach to explaining moral thought and action. *Academy of Management Review, 36(4),* 663–685.

Hannah, S. T., Jennings, P. L., Bluhm, D., Peng, A., & Schaubroeck, J. (2014). Duty orientation: Theoretical development and preliminary construct testing. *Organizational Behavior and Human Decision Processes, 123,* 220–238.

Hannah, S. T., Schaubroeck, J., Peng, A. C., Lord, R. L., Trevino, L. K., Kozlowski, S. W. J., et al. (2013). Joint influences of individual and work unit abusive supervision on ethical intentions and behaviors: A moderated mediation model. *Journal of Applied Psychology*, *98*, 579–592.

Hannah, S. T., Sweeney, P. J., & Lester, P. B. (2007). Toward a courageous mindset: The subjective act and experience of courage. *Journal of Positive Psychology*, *2*(2), 129–135.

Jennings, P. L., Mitchell, M. S., & Hannah, S. T. (2014). The moral self: A review and integration of the literature. *Journal of Organizational Behavior*. Advanced online publication. doi: 10.1002/job.1919

Jonas, K., Boos, M., & Brandstätter, B. (Eds.). (2007). *Training moral courage: Theory and practice*. Göttingen, Germany: Hogrefe.

Kegan, R. (1982). *The evolving self: Problem and process in human development*. Cambridge, MA: Harvard University Press.

Kidder, R. M. (2003). *Moral courage*. New York, NY: William Morrow.

Kihlstrom, J. F., Beer, J. S., & Klein, S. B. (2003). Self and identity as memory. In M. R. Leary & J. P. Tangney (Eds.), *Handbook of self and identity* (pp. 68–90). New York, NY: Guilford Press.

Kohlberg, L. (1976). Moral stages and moralization: The cognitive-development approach. In T. Lickona (Ed.), *Moral development and behavior: Theory, research, and social issues* (pp. 31–51). New York, NY: Holt, Rinehart, & Winston.

Mayer, R. C., Davis, J. H., & Schoorman, F. D. (1995). An integrative model of organizational trust. *Academy of Management Review*, *20*, 709–734.

McCabe, D. L., Butterfield, K. D., & Trevino, L. K. (2012). *Cheating in college: Why students do it and what educators can do about it*. Baltimore, MD: Johns Hopkins Press.

Morrill, R. L. (1980). *Teaching values in college*. San Francisco: Jossey-Bass.

Pascarella, E. T., & Terenzini, P. T. (2005). *How college affects students: A third decade of research* (Vol. 2). San Francisco, CA: Jossey-Bass.

Perry, W. G., Jr. (1981). Cognitive and ethical growth: The making of meaning. In A. W. Chickering & Associates (Eds.), *The modern American college* (pp. 64–84). San Francisco, CA: Jossey-Bass.

Putman, D. (2010). Philosophical roots of the concept of courage. In C. Pury & S. Lopez (Eds.), *The psychology of courage: Modern research on an ancient virtue* (pp. 9–22). Washington, DC: American Psychological Association.

Rest, J. R., Narvaez, D., Bebeau, M. J., & Thoma, S. J. (1999). *Postconventional moral thinking: A neo-Kohlbergian approach*. Mahwah, NJ: Lawrence Erlbaum Associates.

Schaubroeck, J., Hannah, S., Avolio, B. J., Kozlowski, S. W., Lord, R. L., et al. (2012). Embedding ethical leadership within and across organization levels. *Academy of Management Journal*, *50*, 1053–1078.

Schein, E. H. (2010). *Organizational culture and leadership* (4th ed.). San Francisco, CA: Jossey-Bass.

Sweeney, P. J., & Fry, J. (2012). Character development through spiritual leadership. *Consulting Psychology Journal: Practice and Research*, *64*(2), 89–107.

Sweeney, P. J., Thompson, V. D., & Blanton, H. (2009). Trust and influence in combat: An interdependence model. *Journal of Applied Social Psychology*, *39*, 235–264.

Torres, V., Jones, S. R., & Renn, K. (2009). Identity development theories in student affairs: Origins, current status, and new approaches. *Journal of College Student Development*, *50*, 577–596.

Wagner, W. (2011). Consideration in student development in leadership. In S. Komives, J. Dugan, J. Owen, C. Slack, W. Wagner, & Associates (Eds.), *The handbook for student leadership development* (pp. 85–107). San Francisco, CA: Jossey-Bass.

Walker, L. J. (2004). Gus in the gap: Bridging the judgment-action gap in moral functioning. In D. Lapsley & D. Narvaez (Eds.), *Moral development, self, and identity* (pp. 1–20). Mahwah, NJ: Lawrence Erlbaum Associates.

Walker, L. J., & Henning, K. H. (2004). Differing conceptions of moral exemplarity: Just, brave, and caring. *Journal of Personality and Social Psychology, 86,* 629–647.

Winnicott, D. W. (1960). The theory of parent-infant relationship. *International Journal of Psycho-Analysis, 41,* 585–595.

Patrick J. Sweeney is the director of leadership, character, and business ethics initiatives at the Center for Leadership and Character in the School of Business at Wake Forest University.

Matthew W. Imboden is the director of Integrative Academic and Student Services in the School of Business at Wake Forest University and a PhD candidate in higher education at the University of North Carolina at Greensboro.

Sean T. Hannah is a professor of management, Wilson Chair of Business Ethics, and the executive director of the Center for Leadership and Character in the School of Business at Wake Forest University.

New Directions for Student Leadership • DOI: 10.1002/yd

3

This chapter explores the Giving Voice to Values curriculum, one innovative approach to integrating ethics into leadership development. The chapter describes how Giving Voice to Values is being used in educational settings across the globe.

Learning About Ethical Leadership Through the Giving Voice to Values Curriculum

Mary C. Gentile

The call for values-driven leadership in all sectors of our lives has never been louder. We live in an era when all of us, adults and youth, are bombarded on a daily basis—in the press, on the Internet, or on television—with stories of ethical transgression, short-term thinking, and moral shortcuts, surrender to group pressures, or a simple lack of attention to values. For those of us who work in the education arena, the immediate issues are obvious: cheating, plagiarism, bullying, discrimination, and so on.

There have been many calls for the inclusion of ethics and values within the curriculum itself. For example, the University of Texas-Austin distribution requirements dictate that all undergraduates take a certain number of courses that have been "flagged" as containing substantial content around ethical leadership. In my field of business education, the clamor for attention to ethics in the curriculum has been building for decades and has led to accreditation revisions and numerous courses, both required and elective.

However, there is also a need to find ways to weave this sort of personal development into the larger educational environment and institutional culture. If the school context does not reflect, support, and reinforce a commitment to values-driven action, the course content tends to be trumped by lived realities. The question then becomes whether there are approaches and lessons that can be borrowed and adapted from the classroom for use in this extracurricular arena.

In this chapter, we explore an innovative approach to values-driven leadership called "Giving Voice to Values" (GVV) that has been developed and piloted in hundreds of educational and organizational settings across

NEW DIRECTIONS FOR STUDENT LEADERSHIP, no. 146, Summer 2015 © 2015 Wiley Periodicals, Inc., A Wiley Company
Published online in Wiley Online Library (wileyonlinelibrary.com) • DOI: 10.1002/yd.20133

the globe. Although developed as a response to the challenge of transforming management education's approach to ethics in the curriculum, GVV has grown well beyond that original purpose. It is now increasingly seen as a way to transform the larger conversation about values and behavior, with a particular focus upon preparation for *action*. This chapter also includes a number of case examples of cocurricular GVV pilots and applications at both the college and secondary levels.

So What Is Giving Voice to Values?

Giving Voice to Values was developed in response to my frustration with traditional pedagogical approaches to applied ethics, specifically in the business curriculum, and to leadership development. Having worked for a couple of decades in graduate business education, specifically in the ethics, diversity, and leadership areas, I believe that the challenge is not simply a resistance on the part of faculty across the business core curriculum to address ethics and values (as many would argue), but rather it has to do with the manner in which we teach the subject. In fact, I have concluded that part of the reason faculty members in other disciplines (outside of ethics) are often resistant to address values-related issues is due to the same limitations in our pedagogical approach.

Insufficiency of Awareness and Analysis. That is, the traditional approach to applied ethics in business education has been two pronged: we build *awareness* and teach *analysis*. Building awareness dictates that we expose students to case examples of the sorts of ethical transgressions and values conflicts that they might experience in their careers, with the idea that this exposure will make them more likely to recognize such conflicts when they encounter them. This is an important part of ethics education, because many ethical issues are emergent, unclear, or simply go unnoticed; they seem to be a part of doing business, or it seems that no one else sees the problem so perhaps it is not there. However, very often we are quite aware of an ethical challenge (e.g., cheating), and the failure to behave ethically is due to an entirely different set of factors such as time pressure, loyalty to friends, or fear of ostracism. Building awareness is important but not sufficient.

Teaching analysis, on the other hand, is all about developing a systematic and rigorous approach to thinking about and reasoning through various ethical dilemmas. This is typically done by introducing the models of ethical reasoning that are based in philosophy such as utilitarianism, deontology, or virtue-based ethics. Students are exposed to these various models and then invited to analyze a values-conflict by applying each of these lenses to it. Important as it is to be schooled in ethical analysis, this is not a sufficient approach to values-driven leadership development either. By design, these models of ethical reasoning conflict; they allow one to see a situation from various perspectives, recognizing the implications of each possible choice.

NEW DIRECTIONS FOR STUDENT LEADERSHIP • DOI: 10.1002/yd

But they do not definitively identify the "right choice" and they certainly do not provide guidance on implementing a choice, once made.

Although both of these educational objectives—building awareness and teaching analysis—are valuable and essential, they are not sufficient for values-driven leadership development. They treat values and ethics as if the challenge is entirely of the mind, as if we only need to be able to see the problem and decide what to do. However, quite often the most persistent ethical challenges in life occur when most parties are fully aware of them and understand the values at stake, but nevertheless, they still feel unable, uncomfortable, or unprepared to find a way to act on that understanding. They need the opportunity to literally pre-script, rehearse, and refine their implementation plans for addressing the conflict.

Moving to Action.   GVV was developed in order to ask and answer a new question: "Once you know what you think is right, how do you get it done?" GVV goes beyond *awareness* and *analysis* to *action*, providing a set of examples, tools, and a methodology for literally rehearsing and refining, through peer coaching, tactics and scripts, and approaches to values-driven behaviors.

This shift in emphasis is based in both observation and research that suggest, as Pascale, Sternin, and Sternin (2010) expressed it: "It's easier to act your way into a new way of thinking than think your way into a new way of acting" (p. 83). Work in the fields of social psychology, cognitive neuroscience, and even kinesthetics suggests that "rehearsal" is an effective way to influence behavior (Gentile, 2010). And nevertheless, the typical approach to ethics education and values-driven leadership development not only pays scant attention to action, too often it unfortunately albeit unintentionally involves a rehearsal for rationalizing the failure to act. That is, by focusing extensively on so-called ethical dilemmas—the so-called "grey areas"—and by applying the various models of ethical reasoning to them, students can too often walk away with a sense that the "right answer" to ethical challenges is purely a matter of debate and moreover, that there are equally valid arguments on just about any side of the problem. This can unfortunately amount to a sort of schooling for sophistry!

How Does Giving Voice to Values Work?

At the heart of Giving Voice to Values is what we call the "GVV Thought Experiment." We invite participants to engage in a joint creative problem-solving exercise where we posit a values conflict and a protagonist who has concluded what he or she believes is right. Then instead of asking "What would you do?," we ask "What if you were this protagonist? How could he or she act on their values, effectively?"

This exercise is a pedagogical sleight of hand. Instead of spending the discussion in an endless and unresolved debate about right or wrong, the students move right into a sort of action laboratory, a safe space to solve problems, and work together to craft believable, feasible strategies for action. In this way, we remove the fear of seeming naïve or Pollyanna-ish if one espouses a values-driven position. Instead of proving one's sophistication by taking the skeptical position (i.e., "I know what you want me to say and do, but in the real world, it's just not possible"), students can prove their savvy by figuring out how to do the thing everyone says is not possible.

Case Examples.   We support and enable this GVV Thought Experiment by sharing case examples that often have an epilogue where the protagonist actually found an effective way to enact their values. The short-case scenarios conclude at the point where the protagonist has decided what he or she wants to do but needs to craft an action plan and scripts for getting it done. We invite students to work through a template of questions as they respond to the scenarios:

What is the values-based position that the protagonist wants to promote/ achieve?

What is at stake or at risk for all affected parties? (This question is intended not as a prelude to a traditional stakeholder analysis but rather as a way to identify potential influence strategies. That is, if I am worried about the cost of refusing to help my roommate to cheat, perhaps you could help me see ways to say "no" to him or her diplomatically.)

What are the "reasons and rationalizations" (the pushback or objections) the protagonist is most likely to hear when they do try to voice and enact their values? These arguments are often predictable and vulnerable to response if we anticipate them and practice.

What is the best script and action plan for the protagonist? How can we respond to the objections identified here and/or reframe the challenge in a way that is most effective?

Frameworks.   We also identify and share commonly used approaches, tools, frameworks, or "levers" for making persuasive arguments and building support for a values-based position. These tools are based in research on decision-making biases and heuristics, as well as influence and negotiation tactics. And upon reviewing the stories of those who have successfully enacted their values, we have identified a set of principles that appear to enable and support their actions.

Peer Coaching.   Students work in teams to respond to the questions and to craft their best scripts and action plans for the case protagonist. They share those approaches with the rest of the group and all engage in a peer-coaching session. Unlike a traditional adversarial "role play" where the objective is to identify the flaws in the other person's argument, the GVV peer-coaching exercise places all the students on the same side of the question. The process is to identify what is best and seems most likely to be effective in the student scripts and action plans, while also identifying the weaker areas. The peer coaches go on to address the weaknesses they have identified so the entire cohort is engaged in solving the same problem and pushing each other's solutions further.

It should be evident by now that the point of this exercise is not only to come up with usable responses to frequently experienced values conflicts and to rehearse them but also to have the experience of working with one's peers toward a shared values-driven objective.

"A Tale of Two Stories".   Although the GVV Thought Experiment and its focus on action is at the heart of the pedagogy, one of the foundational exercises that often precedes the experience of the pre-scripting and action planning just described is called "A Tale of Two Stories." This exercise is premised on the idea that in their lives students have no doubt encountered situations when their own values conflicted with what they experienced, observed, or were asked to do.

Often it is not easy to align one's own personal values and purpose with those of their classmates, their teammates, their friends, their family, and so on. This exercise is designed to help students identify and develop the competencies necessary to achieve that alignment. The learning objectives are to reflect on their previous experiences at effectively voicing and acting on their values and to discover which conditions and problem definitions empower them to effectively voice their values and which tend to inhibit that action.

"A Tale of Two Stories" has three components: a self-reflection exercise, a small group debriefing, and a large group debriefing. Students recall a time when they encountered a values conflict (a time when they implicitly or explicitly felt pressure to act counter to their own values), and they found a way to effectively act on their values. They record this example and consider a set of questions about what motivated them, what made it easier (the "enablers"), what made it more difficult (the "disablers"), and how they feel about the situation in retrospect. Then they recall a time when they encountered such a values conflict and failed to act on their values.

In the small group debriefing, they share the positive stories and look for commonalities among the enablers and disablers. They do not share the negative stories (both for confidentiality/safety reasons and because we do not want them to imprint on a lot of negative examples), but we do ask them to consider what was different: why they did not act on their values in those instances.

Finally, in the large group debriefing, they discuss commonalities and observations, they generate a list of enablers and disablers, they begin to see that many of the enablers and disablers are common to all of us and form the template for the sorts of groups they wish to be part of, and they also see that some of the disablers are unique to different individuals and have more to do with one's own experiences. That is, the person who is more risk averse may react differently to the person who enjoys risk taking. The key here is that no one personality "type" is necessary for values-driven behaviors, but rather that the approach one takes is best if it is adapted to one's personal strengths and tendencies.

This exercise has a number of outcomes. It establishes that GVV is not about sorting out the good people from the bad; rather we see that we all have values and that we all have acted on them in some circumstances. We are all capable of values-driven behaviors. On the other hand, we all have failed to act on our values at times. The point is to figure out what makes it easier for us to enact our values and to maximize those factors in our lives while minimizing the disablers and to see that there are as many approaches to effectively enacting our values as there are individuals. This exercise is a powerful and accessible way to engage students in the GVV experience. Students realize they have values that they would like to be better able to act upon, and it sets up the GVV Thought Experiment and its pre-scripting, action planning, rehearsal, and peer coaching as a mechanism for responding to their own "felt" impetus to do so.

Possible Applications Beyond the Traditional Classroom

Although GVV was developed as a pedagogical methodology for integrating values and ethics into the curriculum itself, particularly in business education, it has now been expanded, adapted, and used in many other settings as noted previously. In particular, some organizations and educators have seen the potential for applying this approach to institutional values challenges that occur both inside and outside the classroom. Such challenges may relate to cheating, plagiarism, bullying, diversity, sexual misconduct, substance abuse, and personal leadership development. Although the topics and the context are slightly different (that is, it may be about test-taking ethics rather than about the actual questions on the test), the core methodology—asking "how" rather than "whether" to act ethically, providing group opportunities to pre-script and rehearse action plans for values-driven behaviors, sharing the best implementation plans and scripts and engaging in peer coaching to enhance them, and reflecting on one's individual style and abilities in order to build an approach to values issues that plays to one's strengths—remains consistent.

***

GVV and ASPIRE India

Amit Bhatia.   ASPIRE is a social enterprise, based in India and focused on employability, entrepreneurship, and ethical leadership education. Since 2007, ASPIRE has trained over 62,000 students across India, in 100+ institutions, 16 states, and 47 cities.

ASPIRE launched its ethical leadership product, LeadershipPro, in 2012, with an embedded GVV curriculum. Two independent forces led to this development. First, as an Aspen Institute fellow, Amit Bhatia, founder of ASPIRE, experienced a values-based leadership program between 2006 and 2008, which extensively used Socratic dialogue to inspire professionals between 35 and 45 years of age. Second and providentially, Bhatia met Dr. Mary Gentile at the Aspen Institute and attended two workshops in India for the integration of ethical leadership curriculum in business schools. Bhatia was convinced that values-based, ethical, or enlightened leadership must be cascaded down to middle and high school, when adolescents and teenagers are still forming their values and moral compass.

The opportunity presented in 2012 when India's best day school, The Shri Ram School, in a joint initiative with Aspen India, approached ASPIRE to build a values-based leadership program for high schoolers. Because we were dealing with 14–18 year olds, ASPIRE developed an outbound residential program, for 1 to 2 weeks, with 10 threads—Socratic dialogue, case studies, communication skills, soft skills, adventure sports, performing arts, and so on, which focused on ethical leadership, while being fun, meaningful, and memorable. GVV curriculum has been integrated into the case studies segment, and during ASPIRE's flagship 2-week program, participants delve into multiple GVV cases like "A personal struggle with the definition of success," "Be careful what you wish for: From the middle," "The indent for machines: A sugary finale," "The temple encroachment issue," and end with the exercise "A Tale of Two Stories." Contrary to expectations, high school students are equally baffled and relate to the dilemmas on hand, enjoy the debates and contrasting viewpoints and ultimately, not only discover their own moral compass, but also, in Gentile's words, develop and enhance their "moral muscle." The finale, "A Tale of Two Stories," has always been a candid, confessional exercise for students where they talk about cheating, alcohol/drug abuse, ragging and bullying, shop-lifting, and so on; issues that most outrage and entrap them.

Since 2012, India's leading boarding school with over 75 years legacy, The Doon School, and Asia's largest IB school in India, The Oakridge School, are among the leading Indian institutions that have adopted the program and the GVV curriculum. The students get a certificate cosigned by Bhatia and Gentile and as a souvenir, take home the book, *Giving Voice to Values*. The program has consistently received very high student ratings, and has averaged 4.7 on a scale of 1 to 5, where 4 = *very good* and 5 = *outstanding*.

In summary, the balance of in-class and outbound experience, of reflection and experience, has ensured that GVV embedded in Leadership-Pro is inspiring and achieves our collective aspiration—enlightened hearts with a renewed sense of values.

Giving Voice to Values at Ashesi University in Ghana

Rebecca Awuah. In 2008, when I began teaching mathematics at Ashesi University, a young liberal arts college in Ghana, the student body

NEW DIRECTIONS FOR STUDENT LEADERSHIP • DOI: 10.1002/yd

and administration were engaged in an intense conversation about ethics, academic honesty, and the possibility of instituting the first ever examination honor code in a West African university. The event that triggered the campus-wide debate was a request the previous year by the assistant registrar for faculty and university administrators to assist with proctoring end-of-term examinations. The stated mission of the school is to "educate a new generation of *ethical,* entrepreneurial leaders in Africa; to cultivate within our students the critical thinking skills, the concern for others, and the *courage* it will take to transform a continent." If students could not be trusted to take exams without cheating and did not have the courage to hold their peers accountable, the president of the university felt that Ashesi was failing in its core mission. Responses from the broader university community to the possibility of unproctored exams administered under an honor code were varied, but a common fear expressed by students was "I know I will do the right thing, but I don't trust my colleagues." Many students expressed the view that saying "no" when asked by a friend for inappropriate assistance or reporting a colleague if misconduct was observed in the exam room would be too difficult.

It was in this context that I worked with a small group of faculty and administrators to pilot Giving Voice to Values during the 2009 academic year. The university already had a focus on ethics. The liberal arts core curriculum included instruction in the theories and foundations of ethical reasoning, required leadership courses included analysis of the ethical dimensions of complex real-world cases, disciplinary courses asked students to debate contrasting ethical postures within the profession, and conversations about ethics were an intentional part of Ashesi's institutional culture. But Giving Voice to Values added an important new dimension that could potentially help students adhere to an examination honor code: instruction and practice in ethical action, the skills and motivation necessary to speak up and be heard when one's values are in conflict.

Beginning in the fall of 2010, a 5-week Giving Voice to Values seminar was included as part of the liberal arts core for all freshmen. At that point in time, three out of four year groups had, by majority, signed on to an honor code and had been taking examinations without proctors. Although supporting students in adhering to an examination honor code was an early motivation for including Giving Voice to Values in the core curriculum, Ashesi's mission of educating ethical leaders for Africa who have the courage to take action when their values are in conflict has driven the unique implementation of Giving Voice to Values at our university.

Giving Voice to Values at Ashesi takes the framework and guiding principles of the curriculum and contextualizes the course to young undergraduates in the Ghanaian context. Some activities, such as the "Tale of Two Stories," which seeks to generalize enablers and disablers for speaking up, inherently adapt to the culture, place, and age of the students. For example, speaking up to an elder, extended family expectations, and the status quo around police bribery are disablers that consistently come up in our "Tale of Two Stories" discussions. Other activities, such as scripting and role playing have been contextualized by developing cases around values conflicts that students can be expected to face during their undergraduate years. Examples include conflicts around academic honesty, conflicts that arise in student clubs and during internships, and conflicts that arise in relationships. Contextualization is critical for students to care about, integrate, and apply knowledge and skills around ethical action. By rehearsing scenarios, they or their friends will encounter as students rather than values conflicts that may occur later on in the workplace, the university years become a natural learning environment for young people to practice and develop the habit of ethical action.

Having members of staff such as the human resources and finance managers and faculty from different disciplines teach sections of the seminar is a further aspect of Ashesi's contextualization of Giving Voice to Values and one which seeks to model ethical action as a skill for everyone, not a particular area of specialty. And finally, each Giving Voice to Values instructor is paired with an Ashesi alum who cofacilitates the course. Ashesi Alumni bring real-world values conflicts encountered in the Ghanaian workplace to the class discussions, and they offer credible feedback and coaching on scripts and role plays.

In 2013, third-year students were surveyed about their Giving Voice to Values experience as freshman, and the results were encouraging. The juniors reported that they did in fact experience a range of values conflicts in school and in the community during their undergraduate years. And when asked in what way the Giving Voice to Values experience may have been helpful in those situations, more than half of students responded that "GVV helped motivate me to speak up." Based on follow-up interviews and anecdotes, it appears that Giving Voice to Values may be evolving into a norm on campus, a norm in which it feels safer for students to speak up when their values are in conflict, and the decision to speak up will be supported by core group of one's peers.

Voicing Values About Reconciliation and Sport in Sri Lanka

Pippa Grange. The GVV methodology offers a practical, user-friendly, action-based method that is driven by individuals' stories and personal experiences. Its overarching objectives are to turn intentions into actions, empower and enable people to stand up and make a difference, and lead change in their own unique way. This doesn't always need to happen in the classroom, and some rich examples of the approach can be seen in unusual places. I was involved in a sport for development project in Sri Lanka with elite Australian Rules Footballers and several partner groups, including Global Reconciliation, Foundation of Goodness, and Sri Lanka Unites. The project involved taking both indigenous and nonindigenous Australian athletes to completely unfamiliar territory and immersing them in new cultures, so that they might explore their own stereotypes, biases, values, and commitments.

Sri Lanka is a place that has faced much adversity in recent history including 27 years of civil war and the Boxing Day tsunami that devastated its shores in 2004. Among such devastation, many Sri Lankans have been able to find (at least temporarily) solace in sport, especially cricket, and it has been on these level playing fields that some people have been able to find empathy for what each other values and to search within themselves for the voice to express their own values with conviction and confidence.

As our Australian group of athletes interacted with the Sri Lankans over a 9- day period, as teammates, opponents, and coaches on field, and as listeners and storytellers on the sidelines, in the Hindu and Buddhist temples and the Islamic mosques, in the offices of officials and the classrooms of schools and community groups, they started to get an appreciation of the regularity and normality of value clashes between people but more important, the extraordinary benefits of being able to state openly what you believe to be right and then acting accordingly.

We have all been confronted by conflicting values at some point in our lives when we knew something was not right, fair, or just, but something might have held us back from saying or doing something. As the Australian athletes debriefed each night following a Giving Voice to Values type of approach, they reflected on the common barriers that hindered them in their own environments from expressing how they felt and from acting according to their intentions. Some examples of these obstacles that the nonindigenous athletes identified included "just feeling silly" about asking for information about indigenous culture or fear of getting something wrong that might come across as disrespectful, or worse, discriminatory. The indigenous athletes spoke about feeling like they needed to compromise their identity in order to "fit in" to the predominantly "white football world" and not always knowing how to stay true to their own culture and be accepted in the rigid, structured, and routine-based world of elite sport.

Through the use of personal stories, local and international examples, and commentaries, the Giving Voice to Values framework helped to guide these athletes on how to go about voicing and acting on what they believe is right. By considering their own experiences throughout their lives of successfully voicing their values (including on the field of play and in their club roles as athletes and performers), each person was more prepared and empowered to follow through on his or her intentions.

One athlete, a young Tiwi Island man called Jonathan who had not travelled outside of his Australian home before the project, offered two profound examples of success in voicing his values. Jonathan was reserved to say the least at the start of the trip, and by his own admission, a little overwhelmed in the company of some of the other extremely well-known and high-profile footballers around him. This resulted in him adopting a quiet, conservative approach to the group debriefings and reflections in the first few days—however, the conversations about values and actions were having a deep impact on Jonathan.

The first example of Jonathan giving voice to his values was in a small tribal village of the indigenous Sri Lankan Veda people in the Central Highlands. The group had listened to and conversed for some time with the tribal chief about what he and his people cared about and how they had found the courage to voice these values and follow a traditional, yet prosperous life in the face of much adversity in a changing land. As the discussions drew to a close, the athletes exchanged skills (football for archery) and laughter with the local people. Then a senior community member offered a traditional dance as a blessing for us on our journey. We were moved and grateful, and some of us wished we had something other than words to express our gratitude. The usually reserved Jonathan stepped forward in front of the gathering and asked if he could reciprocate with a tribal dance from his own people. His face was bright with conviction, and he proceeded to honor and respect the Veda in his own way, from his own deepest identity and values.

The second example came on the final day of the trip, when the group had gathered to speak to the Australian Consular General in Colombo about reconciliation in Sri Lanka and Australia and the role sport and sports people could play. As we sat in the comfortable surrounds of the Australian Embassy and talked about the symbolism and importance of sport, Jonathan raised his hand and asked a question. He felt that we had spent the 9 days getting a better understanding not only of reconciliation and sport but also of ourselves and how we acted or didn't act when we felt something. Jonathan was an indigenous Australian sitting in the Australian Embassy and told the group that he saw the Sri Lankan flag and the Australian flag, but he did not see the Indigenous flag. He hoped to see that flag in the future. The Consular General thanked Jonathan warmly for pointing out such an omission and committed to immediately changing the situation.

Jonathan expressed later that day how proud and authentic he had felt in raising the question, despite the conflict he felt inside between his deference to authority and conservatism and his passion for the recognition of his own people. The great surprise for him was that he had been clear all along about what he valued, but he had missed so many opportunities to voice his values when he hesitated and lost confidence in unfamiliar company. He was also rewarded by the feedback from all other athletes who had appreciated both his actions and his representation of the group.

The GVV approach helped to equip these athletes with greater courage and skill to act on their most deeply held values in both big and small ways, a lesson they can carry forward for life. For more information on the Sri Lankan reconciliation journey see http://bluestoneedge.com/sri-lanka -united-we-stand.

GVV and Middle School Students

Linda Pryor.   When I first began to learn about GVV, I wondered if middle school students could also benefit from its methods. Could GVV help them think more deeply about those tough situations when they know what the right choice is, but they are not sure how to get it done?

I met with a small group of eighth graders and gave them some background on GVV and explained my interest in it. Together we read through a modified version of "A Tale of Two Stories," reworded for their age. I asked them to reflect on the questions proposed and to meet with me a few days later if they were interested in sharing their answers. The majority of the students returned on the appointed day and we had a great conversation. After they shared some real life situations, I focused a lot of time on this question: What conditions would have made it easier for you to speak/act the way you thought was right?

After some moments of silence, the answers were thoughtful and direct. Time was a frequent theme; time to reflect and think about the outcomes of their choices would have made a difference. They admitted that pausing, taking time to imagine how their choices may play out was not their typical way of approaching their decisions, but they saw it as a behavior that would make doing the right thing easier.

Another big factor that they felt could help would be if they talked to other friends and felt supported by even just one more person in making the right choice. However, one student also worried that in seeking support and talking to others, thus enlarging the number of students aware of the situation; she might bring more gossip and attention, which would make the entire situation more problematic and a bigger challenge for her.

In the end, I have determined that I want these same students to write some real cases with me, situations that ring true for them and that we can share with a larger group of participants. Their thoughtfulness and honesty convinced me that we can put GVV to work with middle school students.

Conclusion

From these examples, it becomes clear that the Giving Voice to Values methodology is robust and flexible across a variety of contexts: academic and extracurricular, athletics, different age and academic levels (middle school, high school, undergraduate, graduate), cultural and geographic diversity, and so on. It also can be adapted for a variety of leadership challenges and opportunities: academic integrity, diversity and inclusion, character development, and personal and professional ethics. As I travel around the world sharing this approach, individuals find new applications: addressing homophobia in business settings, developing strategies for dealing with substance abuse, creating scripts and action plans for resisting cheating, and teaching applied ethics in the formal curriculum.

The promise and the appeal of Giving Voice to Values is both its basis in experience and scholarship, on the one hand, and its intuitive appeal, on the other. It is simple and accessible, yet powerful as a methodology for developing and enabling values-driven leadership at all levels.

References

Gentile, M. (2010). *Giving voice to values: How to speak your mind when you know what's right.* New Haven, CT: Yale University Press.

Pascale, R., Sternin, J., & Sternin, M. (2010). *The power of positive deviance: How unlikely innovators solve the world's toughest problems.* Boston, MA: Harvard Business Review Press.

MARY C. GENTILE is the director of Giving Voice to Values and a senior research scholar at Babson College.

4

This chapter is about a unique partnership between Ravenscroft, a pre-K–12th grade independent school in Raleigh, North Carolina, and the Center for Creative Leadership. Starting in pre-K, Ravenscroft students embark on the Lead From Here initiative that inspires and empowers them to become citizen leaders.

At What Age Should We Begin Developing Ethical Leaders?

Marin Burton, Christopher A. Ward, Colleen Ramsden

On a spring morning at Ravenscroft School, the assistant head of school and a Center for Creative Leadership (CCL) staff member walked into a parents' association meeting. They stood in front of the room and simply asked parents, "What are the skills and competencies you want your children to be equipped with when they leave Ravenscroft?" The parents shouted out words like compassion, ability to work effectively in teams, integrity, ability to work with people from other cultures, and leadership skills. On a flipchart, the facilitators frantically tried to capture all of the hopes and dreams these parents had for their children. Next, the assistant head and the CCL staff member presented the Ravenscroft Citizen Leader Framework. The alignment was clear; what parents had shouted out was represented somewhere in the framework.

In this chapter we explore a new culture of citizen leadership at Ravenscroft School—its origins, strategic approach, implementation strategy, and seven foundational principles of our collaboration. It is hoped that this pioneering work will serve educational communities as they continue to grasp the importance of holistic development for an ever-changing world.

Origins

The origin of Lead From Here is rooted in the convergence of two communities dedicated to catalyzing human development—Ravenscroft School and the Center for Creative Leadership. For both organizations, this partnership is considered a privilege and responsibility to society and the future.

New Directions for Student Leadership, no. 146, Summer 2015 © 2015 Wiley Periodicals, Inc., A Wiley Company
Published online in Wiley Online Library (wileyonlinelibrary.com) • DOI: 10.1002/yd.20134

It is, as is all good education, rooted in an ethic that strives to promote the common good.

In 2010, Ravenscroft was deeply engaged in a new phase of strategic planning as well as getting ready to celebrate its 150th anniversary. Ravenscroft is driven by its mission: "Guided by our legacy of excellence, we will nurture individual potential and prepare students to thrive in a complex and interdependent world" (Ravenscroft, 2014). While identifying strategic objectives to maintain excellence, Ravenscroft's head of school identified a broader opportunity to fulfill their commitment to the school's mission.

As Ravenscroft faculty, staff, and parents reflected on the ethos of their community and the needs of students and society, they also recognized that helping students grow into strong citizens within their local, regional, and global communities was essential. Additionally, the Ravenscroft community, like many top-tier, independent schools, has a long history of shepherding the development of the "whole child" in addition to the academic rigor and excellence that it instills. After decades on that pathway, Ravenscroft was aware of the possibilities in making holistic student development even more strategic and effective. Out of this wisdom a strategic initiative was born—to engage students in leadership and citizenship development.

Eighty-five miles west of the Ravenscroft campus, the Center for Creative Leadership was engaged in a similar purpose. It was founded in 1970, through the Richardson Foundation, to research and develop creative leadership for business, industry, and the benefit of society. The center is one of the primary pioneers in the leadership development field, innovating many of the best practices of leadership development widely employed today. Though its historic focus had been on positional leaders in business and industry, in 2006, CCL started a new initiative—Leadership Beyond Boundaries. This team began to discover, serve, and partner to put leadership development's best practices in the hands of many groups of people who have not traditionally had access to these practices—including young people and low-resource communities worldwide.

The Leadership Beyond Boundaries team has worked with a host of organizations such as the YMCA; Southern Methodist University's Hart Center for Engineering Leadership; business schools in India; nongovernmental organizations in Africa; and the Golden Leaf Foundation of North Carolina. Through this work, the Leadership Beyond Boundaries team identified that the "sweet spot" of its mission was to partner with organizations to help them develop the capacity to bring leadership growth to their communities. Therefore, when Ravenscroft reached out to begin a dialogue with CCL in 2010, the stage was set for both institutions to see the power of a collaborative partnership.

Fueled by CCL research revealing the critical need for preparing young leaders for the future (Van Velsor & Wright, 2012), Ravenscroft and the

Figure 4.1.   Evidence From the Work World

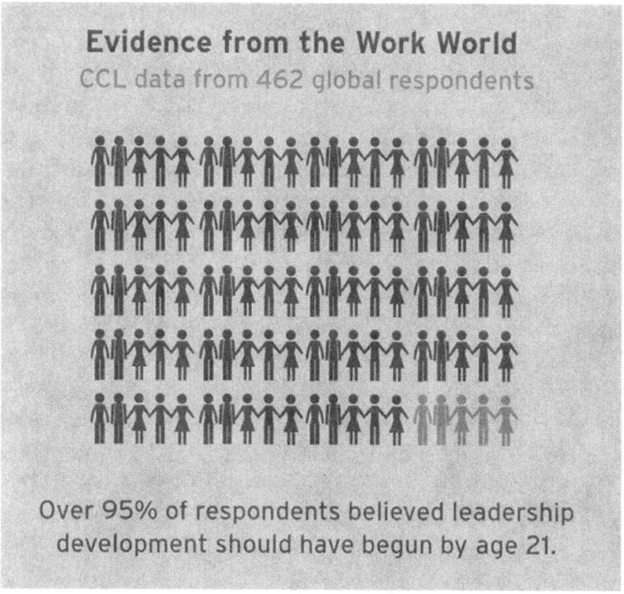

Evidence from the Work World
CCL data from 462 global respondents

Over 95% of respondents believed leadership development should have begun by age 21.

Source: "Expanding the leadership equation: A CCL white paper" by E. Van Velsor, & J. F. Wright, 2012, p. 3. Copyright 2012 by Center for Creative Leadership.

CCL began the discovery phase of collaboration to explore the cultural points of emphasis regarding leadership and citizenship (see Figure 4.1 and Table 4.1).

Ravenscroft worked with CCL to identify the competencies of powerful citizen leaders, which became known as the Citizen Leader Framework. In December 2012, the Ravenscroft Board of Trustees made a commitment to a multiyear collaboration with CCL to design and implement a comprehensive initiative that came to be known as Lead From Here.

Table 4.1   Beginning Leadership Development

At What Age Do You Think Leadership Development Should Begin?

5 years old or younger	21%
Ages 6–10	29%
Ages 11–17	40%
Ages 18–21	7%
Over 21	3%

Source: "Expanding the leadership equation: A CCL white paper" by E. Van Velsor, & J. F. Wright, 2012, p. 4. Copyright 2012 by Center for Creative Leadership.

Comprehensive Approach

The synergy of expertise between Ravenscroft's administration, faculty, staff, and the Center for Creative Leadership's Leadership Beyond Boundaries team was evident very early in the process. Ravenscroft brought decades of expertise in child and adolescent development models, techniques, and educational best practices. CCL's Leadership Beyond Boundaries team brought research and its best practices from the global field of leadership development, which were innovated to empower young people. Both organizations shared expertise in human development and an active and genuine passion to work for the betterment of society.

Entering the process with a high value for systems thinking, and grounded in learning and developmental theories, it became very clear through the discovery phase that, in order to truly develop citizen leaders, a multilayered, multistakeholder strategic approach would be required. Team members recognized that many schools and institutions identified the importance of developing leaders, and a subset of those schools are doing it robustly. But what emerged powerfully through discovery and dialogue was the insight that every child can become a citizen leader.

Clearly, a developmental endeavor of this depth and breadth requires a proportionally robust strategic approach. It is important to note that, from the beginning, Lead From Here was imagined as an initiative that could help *all* students—not just a select few—develop as citizen leaders. There is a strong belief that all humans, regardless of position, age, or background, can participate in leadership and work with their individual strengths and challenges to lead. One of the most obvious ways in which this is exhibited in Ravenscroft's developmental approach is that citizen leadership development begins with the youngest Ravens—in pre-K—and follows a scope and sequence of learning that moves longitudinally through their graduation from the upper school.

The Framework.   The Citizen Leader Framework (see Figure 4.2) is composed of three spheres of citizen leadership, which interact in a Venn diagram. Under each sphere are five citizen leader competencies, which were culled from CCL's leadership, entrepreneurial, and innovative practices and filtered through the particular values and needs of Ravenscroft's students and community.

The first sphere is Leading Self; it includes the competencies Self-Aware, Motivated, Growth-Minded, Resilient, and Accountable. The second is Leading With Others, which includes Empathetic, Collaborative, Communicative, Culturally Inclusive, and Ethical. Finally, Changing Your World includes the competencies Visionary, Strategic, Adaptive, Resourceful, and Reflective. Each of these spheres builds on one another like building blocks, and, simultaneously, they are in constant interaction in the developmental process. At the center of the framework, where the three spheres converge

NEW DIRECTIONS FOR STUDENT LEADERSHIP • DOI: 10.1002/yd

Figure 4.2.   Three Cycles of Leadership and Citizenship at Ravenscroft

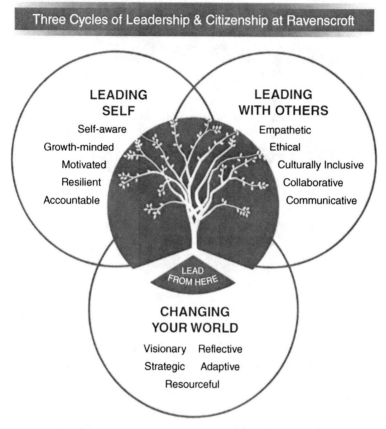

Three Cycles of Leadership & Citizenship at Ravenscroft

LEADING
SELF
Self-aware
Growth-minded
Motivated
Resilient
Accountable

LEADING
WITH OTHERS
Empathetic
Ethical
Culturally Inclusive
Collaborative
Communicative

LEAD
FROM HERE

CHANGING
YOUR WORLD
Visionary   Reflective
Strategic   Adaptive
Resourceful

Source: Ravenscroft Framework adapted from Leadership Beyond Boundaries, 2012, *Why Early Leadership Development?* Retrieved from http://leadbeyond.org/2012/11/13/1878/ and Ravenscroft Citizen Leader Framework, 2014, *Mission, Vision, Values*. Retrieved from http://www.ravenscroft .org/page.cfm?p=1960

is the Ravenscroft Character Tree, a symbol that has been used to represent key character traits within the Ravenscroft community.

   Cycles of Implementation.   At its core, the curriculum map has students cycling through the Citizen Leader Framework three times throughout their Ravenscroft experience (see Figure 4.3). Within each division (lower, middle, and upper) students hear about the entire framework in each grade but target a specific set of competencies at particular ages. Pre-K, kindergarten, and first-grade students will experience lessons focusing on Leading Self. Second and third graders learn about Leading With Others, and fourth and fifth graders focus on Changing Your World. This

Figure 4.3.   The Citizen Leader Framework

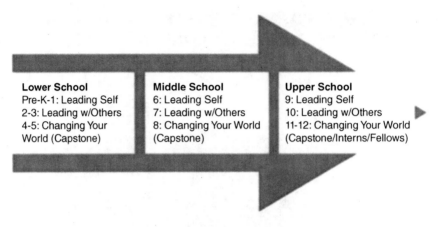

Retreats/Advisory/Classroom/Service Learning/
Out of Class/Out of School

Source: Ravenscroft Board of Trustees Summit 2012. Greensboro: Center for Creative Leadership, 2012.

is not to exclude the rest of the framework but to bring key developmental markers into focus for faculty and students alike. This cycle is repeated in middle school (6th grade—Leading Self, 7th grade—Leading With Others, 8th grade—Changing Your World) and upper school (9th Grade—Leading Self, 10th grade—Leading With Others, 11th and 12th grade—Changing Your World).

Within each learning experience, the curriculum seeks to develop skills, tools, and mindsets that empower students to make the competencies actionable at their age and developmental level. Learning and growth is measured using a range of data collection methods to assess learning that parallels early stages of Bloom's (1956) taxonomy. Curricula should support the students' ability to learn, to clearly articulate, to demonstrate understanding, and to apply the competencies within their lives. Recognizing the importance of developmental stages and increasing cognitive complexity, the curricular scope and sequence enable students to build upon their learning longitudinally. Key artifacts and reflections from each grade level are archived in a student's digital portfolio, which each student customizes and keeps over the years. The online portfolio is being implemented over time, and it creates a space for each student to curate their own learning process with guidance from faculty and staff. In the future students preparing to apply to colleges and write scholarship essays will review their portfolios in order to ground their reflections and ambitions in their concrete developmental journey. It is believed that this portfolio, coupled with the developmental approach, will make way for powerful integration and transfer of learning throughout a student's education, as well as into college and beyond.

Multiple Strategies for Implementation

Developmental change is complex and holistic, and therefore requires a proportional strategic process. Implementation must be both planned and authentic. In order to achieve this, Ravenscroft School has emphasized the following overlapping curricular and cocurricular strategies that engage the majority of stakeholders in the school community.

Direct Instruction.   The Ravenscroft and Center for Creative Leadership collaborative curriculum design team determined that students would develop most effectively if they receive specific, developmentally appropriate instruction on each sphere and competency. Experiential lessons are taught at all grade levels. Through videos, role playing, case scenarios, and activities, the students are given opportunities to exercise their leadership and decision-making skills. No matter what type of lesson occurs, the most important part of the process is the debriefing discussion that happens after the activity. We find when the students have a voice in the discussion, they are more likely to actively participate.

Teachable Moments.   Faculty and staff identify teachable moments within the school day, both within the classroom and outside—on the playground, the rehearsal room, by the water fountain, on the practice field, or in the cafeteria. These are experiences that happen on the spot, where a teacher might stop the regular routine to discuss any given situation. An example that often occurs in lower school is on the playground when one student is left out of a game. The teacher will bring all the children together and discuss the impact the choice had on the student as well as the class community. Some questions the teacher would ask the students to reflect on include: How can I be more aware that others are being left out? What can I do when I notice others are being left out? If I see someone sitting by himself or herself, what could I do? What can I say to others when I feel like someone is being excluded?

We ask the students to "walk in someone else's shoes" and think about how it feels to be left out or different and then take action to prevent it from happening.

Infusion into Academic Curriculum.   When teachers authentically infuse the Citizen Leader Framework into their teaching practices, the competencies come to life. In the eighth graders' culminating project, Ravens in Action, students research a chosen global issue such as poverty, water, pollution, cultural differences, or treatment of women. They bring awareness and recommend solutions about these issues to school community.

The seventh graders go to the Heifer International Global Village in Maryland, where they learn the difference between hunger, malnutrition, and starvation. They are randomly divided into "family groups" tasked with cooking with limited resources on open fires at authentic Kenyan, Appalachian, and Guatemalan homes. These experiences give students an opportunity to think about the impact their actions have on others. They grow in empathy and compassion, and they develop a great appreciation for differences.

Upper school students who are interested in global issues, world languages, and travel to pursue their international dreams, passions, and curiosities have an opportunity to earn an international diploma. Requirements for this diploma include hosting students from other countries, traveling abroad to learn about other cultures and taking specific courses such as Global Issues. The international diploma promotes the Ravenscroft mission by equipping students with the knowledge and habits of mind needed to thrive in our complex and interdependent world. Students traveled to Zambia when Ravenscroft partnered with "Pack for a Purpose" (www.packforapurpose.org) to distribute 500 pounds of supplies, which were donated by students and faculty. A blog post from a student says:

> While we unpacked the suitcases inside the school, the children eagerly lined up and fought to look through the windows at all the new toys and school supplies. Children clutched new pencils and plush animals as they grinned from ear to ear. The pure joy on their faces was infectious. The amount of happiness a single pencil or stuffed animal provided was humbling for the Ravenscroft students to see. After the supplies were distributed, it was time for fun! We danced, played net ball, kicked the soccer ball, played hand games, and had a fantastic time running around with all of the kids; despite the fact that we were from different sides of the world.

Faculty and Staff as Role Models.   A ninth-grade student can learn powerful aspects of citizen leadership by participating in a well-designed lesson, but a much deeper level of change is possible for that student if the lesson is taught by a well-trained Ravenscroft faculty member who embodies citizen leadership. The title of Sizer and Sizer's (1999) book says it all: *The Students Are Watching*. As faculty, staff, and administrators, the most important thing we can do is model for students the importance of making good choices. It is our responsibility to be ever mindful of our words and actions. This is not to say we have to be perfect. As a matter a fact it is important for our students to see us make mistakes, fail, learn, and grow. The lower school guidance counselor shares the importance of this message with faculty. She tells the faculty to let their students see them break an egg. Children often put the adults in their lives on pedestals and think they are infallible. When children see the adults in their lives wrestle with difficult decisions, they are more likely to take risks, be honest about their mistakes, and learn from their experiences.

At an upper school honor council assembly, the entire student body listened as an upper school teacher shared how he made a bad choice in high school and cheated on a test. He explained that even though he was not caught, he knew what he did, and he never forgave himself.

Involving Parents in the Process. It quickly became evident that parent support, understanding, and involvement are key to the successful implementation of Lead From Here.When parents grow in knowledge and practice of the citizen leader competencies and become true developmental partners, the school community can become radically transformed. The Parent Leadership Council was developed in an effort to deepen and accelerate Lead From Here across the Ravenscroft community, especially among Ravenscroft families. The Parent Leadership Council supports efforts to unleash the leadership potential of Ravenscroft students by connecting fellow parents to this exciting and change-making initiative. The roles of the Parent Leadership Council are to develop and support strategies, to engage the parent body in Lead From Here, and to help execute the implementation of parent engagement activities. One example of the Parent Leadership Council engaging other parents was when a fourth-grade parent hosted a leadership luncheon at her home and invited all the parents with fourth-graders to attend. The head of school and assistant head of school were invited to facilitate activities and discussions about Lead From Here. The members of the Parent Leadership Council that were in attendance gave specific examples of how they are using the citizen leader competencies in their homes.

Employing this comprehensive model allows children to be rooted and grow tall within a dynamic, supportive, developmental ecosystem. Recognizing this is not a linear path but one that involves learning, action, and reflection, Ravenscroft students will constantly be exposed to direct instruction, teachable moments both inside and outside the classroom, curricular infusion, adult role models, and parent engagement, which will help them grow and equip them to create positive impact in the world around them.

What We Are Learning

One of the unique components of the Center for Creative Leadership/ Ravenscroft partnership is the ethical beliefs that guide our working relationship. These ethical core beliefs and principles enable us to maintain the spirit of our work with integrity. We believe the world needs ethical renewal. Fostering ethical leaders in the institutions of the world is a significant strategy. We believe that integrating citizen leadership into the fabric of the school is a powerful ethical intervention that is crucial to the holistic human development of young people.

The Center for Creative Leadership/Ravenscroft relationship is collaborative; we see each other as partners. The CCL faculty is on the Ravenscroft campus 3 days a week, and this has played a critical role in our success to date. The collaboration is so pervasive that the Center for Creative Leadership faculty members feel like they are a part of the Ravenscroft staff and

Ravenscroft feels part of a leadership development movement. Interdependence is essential to our work and frees each partner to bring expertise to the table.

We are learning much from our partnership. The following are seven understandings that guide the foundation of our collaboration:

- Leaders can develop as early as pre-K. Themes of being accountable, becoming self-aware, knowing right and wrong, show up very early in a student's learning. We are learning that citizen leader competencies can be taught in developmentally appropriate ways. Learning and developmental theories are core to our approach.
- Leadership is like a muscle that needs to be exercised to get stronger. The skills and competencies of a citizen leader must be practiced over time with increasing complexity. Beginning early is essential for rich and deep learning.
- Citizen leader development is actually an accelerator for academic education. The competencies needed for life outside of the school setting also enhance the academic process. When a student develops resiliency, they are more likely to persist through academic challenges. Developing a vision for the future enables a student to stay focused on what is required to meet that vision. Such competencies prepare individuals to meet the changing needs of our increasingly complex world.
- The best way to effect positive change in students is to engage in an organizational culture change initiative. It is ineffective to teach citizen leadership if the culture does not support what is taught. Therefore, leadership development is required at all levels of the organization and attention to modeling the competencies of the citizen leader is required. Many of us were not intentionally taught these competencies growing up. Everyone is on a leadership development journey. Our leadership development curriculum succeeds in a culture that practices what it is taught.
- Developing leadership competencies requires a variety of participants—students, faculty, administration, staff, board members, alumni, parents. We all benefit from diverse perspectives and working across boundaries. Creating, nurturing, and managing a feedback-rich process also leads to increased impact and shorter learning loops.
- People must engage authentically in the process, and individuals will take different amounts of time to find their authentic engagement. There is an evolution process that must take place in order to start and sustain organizational change. It requires time to affect the whole educational community.
- We have a servant philosophy—we are here to serve others and to meet them where they are in order to affect change. Ultimately, we believe our work is geared toward impacting the common good and for creating positive change in the world.

Lead From Here: Final Thoughts on a Transformational Initiative

Our goal is to provide all Ravenscroft students with the skills, tools, experiences, support, confidence, and humility to excel in college and beyond. Our hope is that students become engaged, citizen leaders in our global community. We believe we can catalyze a sustained, positive impact in our world through the collective impact of the Ravenscroft community.

Horton & Freire (1990) has provided us with a mantra that has guided our work with their book titled, *We Make the Road by Walking*. As much as we would have loved to have anticipated every challenge we would face, we simply could not know what was down the path until we got there. This realization has been a necessary release valve throughout our complex and involved work. Grace and humility must be applied to each stage of this work.

There is great need to maintain perspective and patience when engaged in an organizational change initiative. In order for the change to stick, people must come to accept the change in their own time. It is fruitful to spend time finding ways to connect, build relationships, and give what is needed for people to take steps forward in the journey. In addition, collaboration takes time and it is the path to buy-in and genuine partnership. There are times when it seems easier to "do it ourselves." Continually, we have learned that taking the time to collaborate saves time down the road. More important, it is through the genuine struggle to work together that real commitment is developed. People believe in what they create.

John Ryan, president of the Center for Creative Leadership, stated:

> Communities around the globe are recognizing the tremendous potential we can unleash by preparing all students to become leaders and citizens. CCL is greatly privileged to partner with Ravenscroft on a truly pioneering initiative that will contribute to a better world—our first Research and Innovation Incubator with a pre-k through 12 school. Together, we will create a transformative educational model that will serve Ravenscroft for generations and influence the broader field of education. (J. Ryan, personal communication, May 20, 2014)

References

Bloom, B. S. (Ed.). (1956). *Taxonomy of educational objectives* (Vol. 1: Cognitive Domain). New York, NY: McKay.

Horton, M., & Freire, P. (1990). *We make the road by walking: Conversations on education and social change*. Philadelphia, PA: Temple University Press.

Leadership Beyond Boundaries. (2012). *Why early leadership development?* Retrieved from http://leadbeyond.org/2012/11/13/1878/

Ravenscroft Board of Trustees Summit 2012. Greensboro: Center for Creative Leadership, 2012.

Ravenscroft. (2014). *Mission, vision, values.* Retrieved from http://www.ravenscroft.org/page.cfm?p=9

Sizer, T., & Sizer, N. F. (1999). *The students are watching.* Boston, MA: Beacon Press.

Van Velsor, E., & Wright, J. F. (2012). *Expanding the leadership equation: A CCL white paper.* Greensboro, NC: Center for Creative Leadership.

MARIN BURTON *is senior early leadership faculty and project director at the Center for Creative Leadership.*

CHRISTOPHER A. WARD *is senior early leadership faculty and project director at the Center for Creative Leadership.*

COLLEEN RAMSDEN *is the assistant head of school for academic affairs at Ravenscroft School.*

The science and application of mindfulness is critical for helping leaders to make ethical decisions. The chapter offers three models that educators can use to connect the new science of well-being and mindfulness to ethical behavior.

When Leading With Integrity Goes Well: Integrating the Mind, Body, and Heart

Nance Lucas

Decades of leadership development programs rooted in ethics and moral education focused on the cognitive and character development of leaders. These programs mainly tapped the left side of the brain, which Einstein noted is the rational part of the mind (Culham, 2013). Military academies, business schools, student leadership, and executive education programs all promoted cognitive orientations that were deemed critical for ethical leadership.

"The intuitive mind is a sacred gift and the rational mind is a faithful servant. We have created a society that honours the servant and has forgotten the gift" (Culham, 2013, p. 4). The *faithful servant* as the rational mind prevailed in advancing ethical approaches in leadership. Fortunately, the *sacred gift* of the intuitive mind is slowly making headway in leadership education. Humans overemphasize the parts of the brain focused on conscious verbal thinking (Haidt, 2006), yet we know relational leadership processes require emotional and social functions activated in other regions of the brain.

Advances in neuroscience, positive psychology, and mindfulness studies make the case for uniting the emotional and cognitive dimensions in facilitating leadership development. Recent research reveals that emotions and instincts can trump reason (Haidt, 2006). Cultivating the emotional intelligence of leaders advances Socrates's maxim to "know thyself." Becoming a leader requires the individual to tap the depths of one's inner knowledge and emotional self (Culham, 2013). Too often, we encourage students to be aware of their core values, strengths, and limitations. This level of self-awareness is important for students' leadership development. Exposing students to think more deeply about *who* they are, *how* their

New Directions for Student Leadership, no. 146, Summer 2015 © 2015 Wiley Periodicals, Inc., A Wiley Company
Published online in Wiley Online Library (wileyonlinelibrary.com) • DOI: 10.1002/yd.20135

values were shaped over time, *why* they lead, *how* they affect others (positively and negatively), and *what* kind of leader they want to become are powerful steps in deepening their self-awareness.

What Do We Mean by Mindfulness and Well-Being?

Ellen Langer, a renowned Harvard University psychologist, has been pursuing research on mindfulness since the early 1970s, when taking up such a soft subject in a traditional discipline was risky to one's scholarly career. Langer positions mindfulness as a social phenomenon, paving the way for its connection to ethics and leadership (Langer & Moldoveanu, 2000). Langer and Moldoveanu (2000) define mindfulness as "the process of drawing novel distinctions" (p. 1). They outline four consequences of the mindfulness process: (a) a greater sensitivity to one's environment, (b) more openness to new information, (c) the creation of new categories for structuring perception, and (d) enhanced awareness of multiple perspectives in problem solving.

Other scholars offer similar definitions of mindfulness, making the distinction that an end goal of mindfulness is developing "a limber state of mind" (Langer, 2014, p. 72). Mindfulness means being attuned to your surroundings, living in the moment, being awake and present to gain greater clarity, displaying equanimity, and making quality connections with your environment and others without judgment. Kashdan and Ciarrochi (2013) define mindfulness as

> paying attention with openness, curiosity, and flexibility. In a state of mindfulness, difficult thoughts and feelings have much less impact and influence over behavior—so mindfulness is likely to be useful for everything from full-blown psychiatric illness to enhancing athletic or business performance. (p. 3)

Studies on the effects of mindfulness reveal a positive impact on creativity, enhancing well-being, increasing longevity, increasing productivity, improving memory, reducing stress, and acquiring greater acuteness in focus and attention (Davidson & Begley, 2012; Kashdan & Ciarrochi, 2013; Siegel, 2010). Research by Brown and Ryan (2003) reveals that individuals high on mindfulness scales were better able to formulate their thoughts and direct their behaviors. In summary, the research from neuroscience and neuropsychology provides evidence that the brain can be trained to respond more holistically to thoughts, feelings, and emotions.

Why is developing mindfulness in leaders important? Mindfulness increases leadership presence and helps position individuals to navigate through challenging and chaotic environments with clarity and purpose (Carroll, 2007; Gonzalez, 2012; Kashdan & Biswas-Diener, 2014). It is a lever to deepening inner knowledge and emotional capacity. Although many leaders have highly evolved intellects, they are less equipped on the social side of emotions and relationships (Rock, 2009). When the area of the brain network associated with tasks such as planning, problem solving, and holding information is highly active, the other side of the brain associated with self-awareness and social cognition becomes less active. When leaders spend most of their time on cognitive tasks, their ability to engage more fully in relational leadership is diminished. Mindfulness, when used as a tool for increasing self-awareness and social awareness, can lead to greater capacities for empathy and understanding others' emotions. This is an especially valuable lesson for students to learn. Practicing mindfulness can help students better regulate their emotions, become more attuned to others' emotions and perspectives, and form high-quality relationships.

The Social Change Model of Leadership (SCM) includes seven core values of leadership development (Higher Education Research Institute [HERI], 1996). One of those core values, consciousness of self, includes the components of both self-awareness *and* mindfulness. Embedded in the definition of consciousness of self is an interrelationship between understanding oneself and having the capacity to observe one's behavior and mental states. The SCM makes a compelling case for the importance of students to be aware of what is happening to them and around them—being mindful in the moment. Asking students to reflect on what is occurring, the emotions they are experiencing, and what they are noticing will help them make more informed decisions.

Leadership scholars often debate the question of whether or not Adolf Hitler was a *good* leader. Qualifying this question with an adjective puts a different spin on the response. In some definitions of leadership, Hitler would not qualify as a *good* leader. For example, Komives, Lucas, and McMahon (2013) define leadership "as a relational and ethical process of people together attempting to accomplish positive change" (p. 14). The elements of ethical leadership and leading for positive change embedded in this definition require *both* intellect and social cognition, drawing upon two different networks of the brain (Rock, 2009). Self-regulation is also a key factor in leadership. In examining research on self-regulation and brain functioning, O'Connor, Cooper, Williams, DeVarney, and Gordon (2013) identified three dimensions of self-regulation: positivity-negativity bias, emotional resilience, and social skills. All three components are critical to becoming an ethical leader. A positivity bias offers hope versus the leader having a bleak outlook (positivity bias). Emotional resilience enables the leader to resist peer pressure and do the right thing. Leaders also need to engage well with others (social skills) to accomplish common goals.

Waldman, Balthazard, and Peterson (2011), drawing from neuroscience, explain the importance of understanding coherence as a way to measure the interconnectedness of the areas and functions of the brain and the implication this has for leadership behaviors, including inspirational leadership. As leaders convey values and beliefs and inspire others to act with higher levels of morality and purpose, we would expect to see greater levels of coherence with cognitive tasks typically associated with leadership.

Why Student Leaders Need to Know How the Brain Works

Exposing students to the basics of how the brain works and how to activate areas of the brain will give them increased capacities, such as in controlling their emotions, influencing their leadership presence, and gaining a greater sense of the needs of others in the leadership process (Rock, 2009). Students can learn that the brain has the ability to change both in structure and function over the lifespan. This phenomenon is known as neuroplasticity (Davidson & Begley, 2012). The brain changes in response to activities, experiences, and internal messages. What you feed it and what you pay attention to are the primary shapers of the brain. Through intentional practices of mental exercises, researchers have shown that our brains can be changed (Davidson & Begley, 2012; Ricard, Lutz, & Davidson, 2014). For example, a study conducted by Hölzel et al. (2011), using an 8-week mindfulness and meditation program, showed changes in the gray matter concentration in the brain, affecting regions in emotional regulation, self-referential processing, learning and memory, and perspective taking. These are all critical concepts for students to develop as they learn what it means to lead with integrity.

This research suggests that leadership educators can help students discern signals to avoid ethically inappropriate behaviors (Woollen, 2011). We need to encourage students to see that both spheres of the brain (left and right) are needed to be ethical leaders. It is important to draw on emotions, as well as knowledge and facts, in sorting through tough, complex ethical challenges, and dilemmas.

Models Advancing the Right Side of the Brain

Current research on understanding the right side of the brain has produced three overlapping but discrete models.

Emotional Styles. Research conducted by Davidson and Begley (2012) and drawn from neuroscientific studies revealed six dimensions of emotional styles based on the classification schema of the brain. These emotional styles are on a continuum with individuals having some combination along all six dimensions resulting in a composite score. Our brains can be trained to shift our set points in response to circumstances or conditions (Davidson & Begley, 2012).

The emotional styles include resilience, outlook, social intuition, self-awareness, sensitivity to context, and attention. A series of questions with corresponding scoring is used to determine whether an individual falls closer to the positive or negative end on each dimension. In analyzing the overall composite scores, students can determine how much and in what direction they would like to move their scores. For example, individuals who are slow to recover from setbacks (resilience) may reflect upon ways they can respond differently to regain their emotional equilibrium. Another way students can gain greater insights about their emotional styles is to invite others who know them well to respond to the questions associated with each emotional style. Emotional styles help us understand how we "perceive the world and react to it, how we engage with others, and how we navigate the obstacle course of life" (Davidson & Begley, 2012, p. 225). Students can learn how to move their set points on each of these emotional styles while still staying true to character, enabling them to adapt to particular circumstances or respond more effectively in challenging situations.

Emotional Intelligence.   Daniel Goleman capitalized on the findings that the brain has a circuitry for emotional intelligence (EI) different from cognitive intelligence. In his *Harvard Business Review* article, Goleman (2004) connected effective leadership to emotional intelligence (EI) by emphasizing its five components of self-awareness, self-regulation, motivation, empathy, and social skills. He makes the argument that intellect alone is not sufficient for high-impact leadership. Based on studies of the relationship between emotional intelligence and effective performance, Goleman found that emotional intelligence was twice as important as technical skills and IQ.

Goleman and his colleagues, Richard Boyatzis and Annie McKee, (2002) leveraged this discovery by connecting emotional intelligence with leadership development. How one executes leadership is also connected to the emotional equation of the brain's function and networks. They argue that the emotional impact of leaders and the resonance they create is more powerful than leaders' intellect (Goleman et al., 2002). They describe resonant leaders as being "in tune with those around them. This results in people working in sync with each other, in tune with each other's thoughts (what to do), and emotions (why to do it)" (Goleman et al., 2002, p. 19).

Although all five skills of emotional intelligence are critical in the leadership process, self-awareness, self-regulation, and empathy serve as fundamental concepts of what it means to lead with integrity and moral purpose. Similar to how we can enhance our emotional styles, the five skills of emotional intelligence can be learned (Goleman, 2004). Students, in particular, could be challenged to grasp the full range of their EI skills given where they are in developing their leadership identity. The emotional intelligence model has promise in helping students understand not only their core values and leadership motivations, but also how their values affect or influence others.

Building on Goleman's work, Shankman and Allen (2008) offer a similar framework designed for college students—Emotionally Intelligent Leadership (EIL). EIL includes three dimensions of emotional intelligence that serve as facilitators of leadership development: consciousness of context, self, and others (Shankman & Allen, 2008, p. 5). Although their model includes a list of 21 capacities of emotionally intelligent leadership, the premise of finding balance among these three dimensions of context, self, and others is key in promoting ethical leadership. Students can benefit from using these three dimensions as guides for resolving ethical dilemmas. Educators can use case studies to facilitate discussion on critical incidents experienced by students to illuminate the role context plays in decision making; how students' emotions, feelings, and reactions affect their leadership effectiveness; and how their relationships with others influence the leadership process.

The SCARF Model.   David Rock (2009) formulated the SCARF model, which outlines the five domains of social experience the brain responds to in reward or threat modes. These five domains are *status, certainty, autonomy, relatedness*, and *fairness*. During any emotional or interpersonal interaction, the brain responds away (threat) or toward (reward) one of these five domains. Leaders can trigger reward or threat modes in others along each of these five components of SCARF.

In the context of ethical leadership, a leader can accentuate publicly the positive examples of team members who walk their talk (status), provide clarity in roles and expectations of colleagues and associates (certainty), empower others to assume authority and responsibility for decisions (autonomy), create and sustain relationships with others (relatedness), and treat others with fairness and respect (fairness). Equally important for leaders is to know how to respond along these dimensions when others feel threatened (i.e., threats to status, uncertainty, competition) and how to shift attention from threat to reward states (Rock, 2009). All five dimensions can be used to analyze and resolve ethical dilemmas and to better understand how individuals can lead with authenticity.

The SCARF model has prediction, regulatory, and explanatory benefits in understanding the impact one has on others and vice versa (Rock & Cox, 2013). Leaders can use this model to gain insights on how to minimize negative emotions and maximize positive emotions during an interaction or circumstance. In addition, leaders can apply the model as a strategy to regulate their emotions and to glean greater insights and learning after an interaction.

How to Apply Mindfulness Models in Practice

Many organizations are adopting the science and application of mindfulness as a way to enhance employees' and members' well-being, productivity, satisfaction, and engagement. All of these factors connect with what it means to lead with integrity and how teams and leaders can wrestle with complicated ethical dilemmas and advance core values and principles with clarity and conviction. How leaders engage with others is a fundamental measure of their character. Students can learn how to increase their capacity to respond to their own emotions as well as to the emotions of others. More important, by becoming more aware of their different emotional styles and practicing the five components of emotional intelligence, students can learn how to communicate more effectively and how to make better decisions. The SCARF model can be used as a heuristic and developmental tool for everyone engaged in the leadership process.

A proliferation of organizations are applying evidence-based practices from the findings of neuroscience and positive psychology, for both practical and noble reasons. Google sponsors mindfulness classes and workshops inside the company for employees. Google's premise is that if you start with focusing on employees' self-knowledge and their inner world, they will be better equipped to change the world. Employees are given the space to explore what it means to live a good life and how that translates seamlessly in their work and personal settings. Concepts such as compassion, empathy, love, and other positive emotions along with the development of social skills are embedded in Google's training programs (Tan, 2012). The creator of this program, Chade-Meng Tan, holds the title at Google as the "Jolly Good Fellow" with a job description of enlightening minds, opening hearts, and creating world peace.

General Mills created a Mindful Leadership Program with proven results—89% of employees report having increased skills in listening and 88% gaining greater clarity in making decisions. Other organizations that have integrated mindfulness education and practices include Target, Aetna International, eBay, Twitter, Ford Motor Company, Green Mountain Coffee Roasters, Apple, and Plantronics (Hunter, 2013).

These examples can be used as case studies for students to analyze how others are applying these concepts in leadership and to understand the impact these practices can have on employees and leaders. They can witness how leaders use mindfulness applications to enhance their creativity in approaching problems that have ethical themes while improving the quality of workplaces.

Implications for College Educators

Although leadership courses and cocurricular leadership programs are the obvious vehicles to facilitate students' learning on the connections between leadership and the science and application of mindfulness and well-being, these insights and practices must begin with educators themselves. Exposing students to the intellectual foundations of mindfulness and well-being is just as important as modeling this work ourselves, inside and outside the classroom. Transforming the classroom and other nonacademic environments into laboratories where students can learn to apply and practice these constructs is a key to inspiring our graduates to live lives of integrity. Universities and colleges are positioned to integrate well-being and mindfulness across the curriculum beyond leadership development programs.

These are life skills that can be taught, learned, and applied to students majoring in any subject matter.

There are a number of evidence-based mindfulness practices suited for students and educators, ranging from practicing gratitude, focused attention exercises, compassion and loving kindness meditation. Educators can integrate these concepts into existing courses and programs or create new ones that provide a substantial focus on bridging science with application while equipping students with tools to apply in their own lives.

Using the models presented in this chapter (emotional styles, emotional intelligence, SCARF) provides students with frameworks to develop their own competencies and efficacies. As students practice these concepts, they will be better prepared to facilitate the well-being of others.

Conclusion

We live in an era characterized as having major disruptions and fast-paced systemic changes requiring a different way of preparing individuals and teams for responsible leadership. When faced with tough ethical dilemmas and when attempting to advance ethical principles in the face of adversity, we need leaders and change agents to remain whole, to calm the forces, and bring greater clarity and creativity into their decision-making processes. We need more compassionate responses to human suffering and higher levels of collaboration and shared leadership in facilitating change for positive outcomes. The challenges of world conflict and intractable social inequities present a compelling case of why this new frontier of mindfulness and well-being is like receiving a sacred gift to complement the faithful servant.

References

Brown, K. W., & Ryan, R. M. (2003). The benefits of being present: Mindfulness and its role in psychological well-being. *Journal of Personality and Social Psychology, 84*, 822–848.

Carroll, M. (2007). *The mindful leader: Awakening your natural management skills through mindfulness meditation.* Boston, MA: Trumpeter Books.

Culham, T. E. (2013). *Ethics education of business leaders. Emotional intelligence, virtues, and contemplative learning.* Charlotte, NC: Information Age Publishing, Inc.

Davidson, R. J., & Begley, S. (2012). *The emotional life of your brain: How its unique patterns affect the way you think, feel, and live—and how you can change them.* New York, NY: Hudson Street Press.

Goleman, D. (2004). What makes a leader? *Best of Harvard Business Review 1998* (pp. 82–91). Boston, MA: Harvard Business Review Press.

Goleman, D., Boyatzis, R., & McKee, A. (2002). *Primal leadership: Learning to lead with emotional intelligence.* Boston, MA: Harvard Business Review Press.

Gonzalez, M. (2012). *Mindful leadership: The 9 ways to self-awareness, transforming yourself, and inspiring others.* Mississauga, Ontario: John Wiley & Sons Canada, Ltd.

Haidt, J. (2006). *The happiness hypothesis: Finding modern truth in ancient wisdom.* New York, NY: Basic.

Higher Education Research Institute [HERI]. (1996). A social change model of leadership development (Version III). Los Angeles, CA: University of California.

Hölzel, B. K., Carmody, J., Vangel, M., Congleton, C., Yerramsetti, S. M., Gard, T., et al. (2011). Mindfulness practice leads to increases in regional brain gray matter density. *Psychiatry Research: Neuroimaging, 191*(1), 36–43.

Hunter, J. (2013, April). Is mindfulness good for business? *Mindful,* 52–59.

Kashdan, T. B., & Biswas-Diener, R. (2014). *The upside of your dark side: Why being your whole self—not just your "good" self—drives success and fulfillment.* New York, NY: Hudson Street Press.

Kashdan, T. B., & Ciarrochi, J. (2013). *Mindfulness, acceptance, and positive psychology: The seven foundations of well-being.* Oakland, CA: Context Press.

Komives, S. R., Lucas, N., & McMahon, T. (2013). *Exploring leadership: For college students who want to make a difference* (3rd ed.). San Francisco, CA: Jossey-Bass.

Langer, E. J. (2014). *Mindfulness: 25th anniversary celebration.* Boston, MA: Da Capo Press.

Langer, E. J., & Moldoveanu, M. (2000). The construct of mindfulness. *Journal of Social Issues, 56*(1), 1–9.

O'Connor, M., Cooper, N. J., Williams, L. M., DeVarney, S., & Gordon, E. (2013). Neuroleadership and the productive brain. In D. Rock & A. Ringleb (Eds.), *Handbook of neuroleadership* (pp. 481–490). Lexington, KY: NeuroLeadership Institute.

Ricard, M., Lutz, A., & Davidson, R. J. (2014, November). Mind of the meditator. *Scientific American, 311*(5), 39–45.

Rock, D. (2009). *Your brain at work: Strategies for overcoming distraction, regaining focus, and working smarter all day long.* New York, NY: HarperCollins.

Rock, D., & Cox, C. (2013). SCARF in 2012: Updating the social neuroscience of collaborating with others. In D. Rock & A. Ringleb (Eds.), *Handbook of neuroleadership* (pp. 329–350). Lexington, KY: NeuroLeadership Institute.

Shankman, M. L., & Allen, S. J. (2008). *Emotionally intelligent leadership: A guide for college students.* San Francisco, CA: Jossey-Bass.

Siegel, D. J. (2010). *Mindsight: The new science of personal transformation.* New York, NY: Bantam Books.

Tan, C. M. (2012). *Search inside yourself: The unexpected path to achieving success, happiness (and world peace).* New York, NY: HarperCollins.

Waldman, D. A., Balthazard, P. A., & Peterson, S. (2011). The neuroscience of leadership: Can we revolutionize the way that leaders are identified and developed? *Academy of Management Perspectives, 25*(1), 60–74.

Woollen, B. (2011). Investment risk and the mind of the financial leader. *Consulting Psychology Journal: Practice and Research, 63*(5), 254–271.

NANCE LUCAS *is an associate professor at New Century College at George Mason University. She also serves as the executive director of the Center for the Advancement of Well-Being.*

6

Learning from ethical failures is critical for overall character development as well as an important aspect in the formation of student leaders. This chapter examines types of ethical failure that students often confront in college. The author includes a personal moral failure that occurred when he was a student leader.

Making Moral Mistakes: What Ethical Failure Can Teach Students About Life and Leadership

Jon C. Dalton

Confronting a Moral Failure in College

When I was a junior in college in the 1960s, I was elected president of my fraternity. I was proud to be elected to the leadership role and wanted to prove to others and myself that I could be an effective leader. As president, I presided at house meetings and formal activities and served as spokesman for the fraternity. On one occasion I was called upon to inform a prospective student member that he could not pledge our fraternity because of a restriction against accepting individuals of the Jewish (and other non-Christian) faith. At the time I did not know that such a restriction existed and will always remember the experience of sitting down with the young man to tell him he could not be a member of the fraternity and why.

I felt an inner conflict over that fraternity policy, which I did not believe in, and I felt guilt about what I had to tell the young man. But, in the end, I concluded I had to follow the rules of the fraternity and do my duty as president to uphold those rules. What could have been an important personal opportunity to speak out against religious discrimination in my fraternity and demonstrate ethical leadership was lost because of my moral insensitivity and lack of courage. As an old man looking back, I wonder how I could have acted in such a morally abhorrent manner. After all these years it is still embarrassing to admit to such behavior especially in a public way. But that incident burned a mark in my conscience that has remained with me and is a persistent reminder about the challenges of ethical leadership, as well as my own capacity for ethical failure. I believe that that experience of

New Directions for Student Leadership, no. 146, Summer 2015 © 2015 Wiley Periodicals, Inc., A Wiley Company
Published online in Wiley Online Library (wileyonlinelibrary.com) • DOI: 10.1002/yd.20136

ethical failure in my youth was pivotal in my own moral development as a leader, and I am convinced that ethical failures have much to teach us and the students we serve about moral maturation and ethical leadership.

In this chapter we explore the nature of ethical failures that students often experience in college. We discuss three important reasons why ethical failures are so common during the college years and how such failures can promote moral growth and ethical leadership skills. Finally, we examine six specific lessons that students can learn from ethical failures and how such lessons can be incorporated into leadership education.

Ethical Failure in College

There are a number of reasons why, sooner or later, students are likely to experience ethical failure during the college years. The college environment inundates undergraduate students with so many new ideas, values, beliefs, and behaviors that frequently pose significant ethical challenges and conflicts for them. Moreover, many students confront these challenging circumstances at a time of heightened vulnerability in life when they may lack sufficient knowledge and experience to make mature and independent moral decisions. Thus, the circumstances of contemporary collegiate life and the limited life experience of many college students create conditions in which ethical failures are very likely to happen.

For these reasons it may well be argued that the college years are some of the most ethically challenging periods of life because of students' encounters with so many moral conflict issues at such a vulnerable point of developmental transition. Consider the range of ethical issues that college students encounter in contemporary college life: academic cheating; alcohol and drug use and abuse; racial, ethnic, and sexual bias and discrimination; sexual harassment and assault; friendships and intimacy; religious conflicts; finding a sustaining life purpose and career; and staying healthy and fit. Sharon Parks (2000) argued that college life has become so challenging for students that many of them will experience "shipwrecks" along the way: they become so overwhelmed by the challenges confronting them that they may experience the loss of meaning and purpose. Smith, Christoffersen, Davidson, and Herzog (2011) observed that young adulthood is a time beset with problems, difficulties, confusions, and misplaced values and devotions. This time in life is all the more complicated, Smith et al. noted, because young adults often have shallow and superficial notions of right and wrong.

Ethical failures are especially common in college, because college *invites* moral failures by pressing students to take moral positions; make ethical choices; take responsibility; and render moral judgments about issues of fairness, justice, responsibility, good and evil. In college, students are encouraged to move outside their comfort zones. Yet with every such venture there is a risk of failure. Educators try to persuade students that they must *un*learn the admonition that it is bad to make mistakes, so that they can be more open and reflective about what failures can teach them.

Because learning in college so actively encourages moral and intellectual exploration and testing, it is not surprising that the services and resources of college life are usually structured to accommodate student failures. A variety of safety- net systems are provided to help students cope with failures. Counselors, advisers, mentors, advocates, and other helpers are ready to assist students who run into trouble. Colleges and universities are designed to be forgiving places where undergraduate students are given second chances and allowed to learn from their mistakes. Of course not all ethical failures can be easily forgiven, but even with the most serious mistakes the purpose of college discipline is constructed not to be punitive but corrective. Colleges and universities recognize that failure can be a powerful source of motivation for students to learn and grow, and college life should be structured in ways to facilitate this educational process.

If youth is such a crucial time for moral exploration, and college life does actively foster and support ethical self-examination, why is so little attention given to the learning and growth gained from the study of ethical failures? Why is there so much hesitancy in actively and purposefully helping students to confront their ethical failures? Because collegiate environments are constructed to encourage students to explore moral and ethical issues and sometimes fail, why are we not more intentional in helping them to cope with and learn from the failures they do encounter?

One reason for such reluctance is that dealing with students' ethical failures can be a messy and difficult business. The ethical failures of students are often highly personal and painful. Faculty and staff often feel uncomfortable dealing with such personal issues in their students' lives and prefer to leave these matters to counselors, advisers, and others with more time and greater expertise.

Another reason for such reluctance is that there is so much emphasis placed upon "success" and "achievement" in higher education today. Any attention given to "failure" may appear to send a contrary message. Many colleges and universities today use the term "success" as both a benchmark educational outcome, as well as an organizational framework for educational and student services. Perhaps the reluctance to focus on learning from ethical mistakes is related to the mistaken assumption that failure is a poor teacher and a negative model for learning.

Educators may also avoid a focus on ethical failure, because any effort to confront ethical failures, especially one's own, requires considerable personal candor and courage. Honestly facing one's moral mistakes can be, as it was for me, a very unpleasant task. Moreover, in the teaching of ethics people are drawn to the use of positive moral exemplars, heroes, and heroines in their efforts to teach about ethical leadership. This approach so often misses, however, the unexpected insights that reflection on moral mistakes can contribute in the formation of exemplary character.

Let us examine some of the reasons that ethical failures are likely to occur in the college environment and how these insights can help us to understand why ethical failure is so common in college and so important in the development of ethical leadership.

Three Primary Reasons for Ethical Failure in College

1. Ignorance or insufficient knowledge
2. Peer pressures
3. Self-interest

Certainly many other reasons and factors are involved in the context of actual ethical failures, but these three reasons seem to be especially relevant and important in understanding why and how college students make ethical mistakes. These three primary causes for ethical failures interact and overlap in the real lives of students. It is difficult to completely separate them. It is useful to consider them independently in order to gain a clearer perspective on some of the most significant ways in which students make ethical mistakes in college.

It should be noted that the term "ethical failure" refers to moral situations in which students act in unethical ways. The situations of ethical failure in which we are especially interested in this chapter include two types: (a) situations in which students *knowingly* choose to act in unethical ways and (b) situations in which students strive to do the right thing but fail. In the first circumstance students choose to act in ways that they have reason to feel are wrong but do so anyway for a host of reasons including pressure, self-interest, fear, or other motivations. The second circumstance includes situations in which students behave in hurtful or morally irresponsible ways but do so largely through ignorance or incomplete knowledge. They do not *knowingly* do the wrong thing but fail ethically for other reasons. Consequently, this definition of "ethical failure" includes both intentional and unintentional behaviors that cause harm or hurt to others. It is possible, of course, to define "ethical failure" in other ways, to exclude unintentional hurtful behaviors but this definition is most useful for understanding how moral failures occur in the college setting and what can be learned for the purposes of leadership development.

Ignorance or Insufficient Knowledge.   College students often make moral mistakes simply because they lack sufficient awareness of the ethical issues and conflicts involved in situations. Ignorance or insufficient knowledge of the complexities of moral situations is especially a problem for those college students who are young and inexperienced with complex life situations. For example, students may use racist or sexist language that is deeply offensive to others without fully realizing the hurt they have caused. Such behavior can be, at least in part, an ethical failure resulting from ignorance or incomplete knowledge. Despite the increasing ethnic and racial diversity of most college campuses today, many college students still have had very limited exposure to others who are different from themselves and may make some moral mistakes due, at least in part, to their lack of experience and knowledge.

In a similar way, it has been my experience that students sometimes violate academic honesty rules due to insufficient knowledge about what constitutes forms of cheating behavior in college. For example, many students are accustomed to studying together in high school for tests and other class assignments and do not recognize that such collaboration may be prohibited by college academic honesty guidelines.

College is also a time of experimentation with many behaviors, and alcohol and drug use are the most common. Many moral mistakes are made by students when they abuse drugs and exceed the moral and social restraints that usually guide their lives. In these college situations, students may fail ethically, because they lose control of the moral compass that helps them to determine right from wrong.

In other situations, students may recognize what is the right thing to do, but they lack experience in how to act on what they know to be right. Aristotle (2011) argued that virtue is acquired through the habituated behavior of doing the right thing. Ethical behavior requires practice as well as sensitivity and recognition. This is one of the reasons why many students "miss the moment" in critical ethical situations. They may have a strong sense of what is right to do but they lack the experience of how to move from conviction to action in their ethical leadership. A key component of ethics education should be to help students to learn to identify the ethical implications of their actions (Bazerman & Banaji, 2004). The opportunity to examine the process of ethical decision making and action can help students avoid ethical failure by providing them with the skills needed to move from moral conviction to action.

Unintentional ethical failures due to ignorance or insufficient knowledge can be just as injurious as intentional acts of unethical behavior. However, although their consequences can be just as damaging, there is reason to argue that ethical failures due to ignorance and inexperience are more forgivable because of the lack of intent to harm or violate others. Moreover, in institutions of higher learning there is usually an acknowledgement of ignorance and inexperience in many domains of a student's learning and development. However, because ethical failures based on ignorance and inexperience are so common, students are often inclined to use this reason as an excuse for ethical failure in order to avoid moral culpability.

Peer Pressures.   Perhaps the greatest influence on ethical failure in the college environment is the college peer culture. Astin (1993) observed that the student's peer group is the single most potent source of influence on growth and learning in college. Smith et al. (2011) noted that in order to understand the decisions and actions of young adults, we must be able to understand the social contexts in which students' lives are embedded. The influence of peers serves to shape ethical norms and standards in students' beliefs and values and can lead to some of the most serious ethical failures students experience in the college environment, especially when students lack the strength of character to resist peer pressure. Peer culture derives its power from its role in granting and denying social approval and recognition to students at a pivotal time in their lives.

It is important to note that student peer culture is different from institutional culture (Dalton & Crosby, 2010). The two domains overlap in the college environment but have significant differences. Institutional culture typically places great emphasis on studying, responsible behavior, respectfulness, diligent work and ethical integrity. On the other hand, student peer culture places a strong emphasis on social competence, fun and friendship, and social graces (Feldman & Newcomb, 1969). Moffatt (1989) observed that for many students college was primarily about fun and freedom from the authority of adults.

The idea of "peer culture" as a theoretical construct is not a new one; it began with Theodore Newcomb's work in 1943 (Milem, 1998). In a number of ethical issues, the peer culture "trumps" the moral influences of the institutional culture through the peer socialization process, which is often more powerful and engaging. Feldman and Newcomb (1969) suggested that student culture can act as a counter influence to colleges' efforts. Thus, college peer culture often serves to mediate and interpret the moral messages, values, and admonitions of the institutional culture. For example, a campus peer culture that condones and even celebrates alcohol use will often modify and moderate institutional efforts to reduce alcohol abuse.

The norms and standards of peer culture have great influence over student concerns about friendships, identity, sexual intimacy, social life, and independence. Peer culture promotes particular moral attitudes, values, and behaviors that may run counter to the personal moral beliefs of students and often tests their moral convictions (Dalton & Crosby, 2010).

Sexual assault on campus is another serious student behavioral problem in which the social influences of the college peer culture often contradict and override the moral and disciplinary efforts of institutions. Despite considerable institutional efforts to reduce the problem (e.g., educational programs, hotlines, training of police and administrators, enhanced campus security, bystander training, victims' advocates, Take Back the Night events, etc.), rates of sexual assault have not declined over the past 5 decades (Armstrong, Hamilton, & Sweeney, 2006). Too often the college peer culture promotes sexual stereotypes and behaviors that demean and even threaten women. Peer culture influences can encourage sexual aggressiveness by promoting expectations that student partygoers drink heavily and that women should defer to men's wishes and impulses (Armstrong et al., 2006).

Self-Interest.   We include self-interest as a primary reason for moral failure in the college environment because of the important role that egocentrism plays in the psychology of human behavior and in the maturation and identity development of young adults. The human development process begins with a primary concern for egocentric needs, and much of the maturation process in life is concerned with learning to balance self-interest with the needs and interests of others. Indeed, much of the focus in the study of ethics is finding the right balance between freedom (self-interest) and responsibility (obligations to others). The tension between self and others is especially stressful during the period of late adolescence when the task of identity development often forces a clarification of the relationships between self and others.

The college years can be a very self-centered time for young people because many are experiencing expanded personal freedom and independence. They are encouraged to explore, to find themselves, to "do their own thing," and to enjoy one of the best times of their lives. Much has been written about generation "me" (Howe & Strauss, 2000), referring to the millennial generation, and the advantages and praise they have received. Many have been encouraged to believe they are the "best and brightest" and therefore entitled to many of the advantages they enjoy. It is not surprising that ethical decision making and behavior can be strongly influenced in college by self-serving motives and influences. This can be seen in the common response given by students who are caught cheating in college: "Everyone cheats; I had to cheat to stay competitive."

What Students Can Learn From Ethical Failure

Ethical failure can be a powerful teacher, and the following are some of the most important lessons to be learned.

- *Ethical failure can reveal our moral ignorance.* Ethical failures have a way of revealing, sometimes in a glaring manner, how little we know and how unprepared we are to manage some moral conflicts. Thus, ethical failures can provide powerful teaching moments in which we confront our intellectual and moral limitations. If students do not seek to avoid or hide from them, ethical failures can help to deepen their understanding of moral issues and prepare them to act more responsibly in challenging ethical situations.
- *Ethical failure can sear our souls.* Failing in situations that define our moral character can be wrenching, soul-searching occasions. Such experiences have the emotional power to make learning deep and lasting. Students' learning is enhanced when they feel a strong emotional connection to the lessons of leadership.
- *Ethical failure can reveal to students the pervasive and often subliminal influence of peers.* An honest examination of ethical failures can help college students to recognize the overt and subliminal influences of peers on their attitudes, beliefs, and values. It is very difficult for college

students to be objective in their recognition of peer group moral influences, since they are so heavily immersed in peer culture. This is especially true when students participate in small, homogeneous groups such as social fraternities, sororities, clubs, and organizations. Learning how to distinguish and affirm personal values over the social and moral influences of powerful peer groups is a key task of leadership development.

- *Ethical failure can open a window to our hidden self.* Ethical failure can provide a moral "selfie" that reveals our own propensities to act in ways that serve our own self interest. A candid examination of self-centered interests and motives in situations of ethical failure can help to unmask our hidden selves and reveal a more honest and realistic appraisal of one's strengths and weaknesses in ethical situations. Effective leadership requires an honest appraisal of personal biases and the ability to prevent them from inappropriately influencing moral judgments and actions.
- *Ethical failure can teach students to think forward.* Experiencing failure can teach students to anticipate and plan for the likelihood of failure in leadership tasks. Some leaders advocate the use of forward thinking, an examination of what might go wrong before it goes wrong. Forward thinking is a leadership strategy in which one imagines that a project or organization has failed and then works backward to determine what factors contributed to the failure. Building in formal opportunities to consider the possibilities of failure can serve as a corrective for being overconfident and discounting real possibilities of failure.
- *Ethical failure can be a friend.* Failure can offer students candid and personal insights on difficult leadership issues that help them to be more perceptive and prepared. Like a good friend, failure can reveal truths about ourselves that make us more open and authentic. The challenge in learning from failure is overcoming the reluctance to admit our own weakness and mistakes. It requires considerable self-confidence and honesty to accept failure. But the ability to admit failure can provide valuable insights in the development of effective leadership.

Conclusion

As I look back on the personal ethical failure I described at the beginning of this chapter, I find myself asking if I would have acted differently had I the benefit of ethical leadership lessons and perspectives described above. Would it have made a difference in how I treated that young man seeking fraternity membership? If I had had the opportunity to learn more about religious differences and the problems of bias and discrimination would it have made me more aware and sensitive about the ethical situation I confronted and the decisions I made? Would having the capacity to more candidly acknowledge and identify my own self-serving motives and biases in the situation have helped me to do the right thing?

Of course I cannot fully know the answers to these questions but I think the added knowledge, practice, and insights in dealing with ethical conflicts would have been very helpful. I believe I would have acted differently, more responsibly. I do know that my ethical failure from so long ago proved to be a powerful factor in my own moral growth and leadership development. Helping college students to confront and learn from their ethical failures can provide transformative lessons in their development as ethical leaders.

References

Aristotle. (2011). *Nicomachean ethics, Book II* (R. C. Bartlett & S. D. Collins, Trans.). Chicago, IL: University of Chicago Press.

Armstrong, E. A., Hamilton, L., & Sweeney, B. (2006). Sexual assault on campus: A multilevel, integrative approach to party rape. *Social Problems, 53*(4), 483–499.

Astin, A. W. (1993). *What matters in college: Four critical years revisited.* San Francisco, CA: Jossey-Bass.

Bazerman, M. H., & Banaji, M. R. (2004, June). The social psychology of ordinary ethical failures. *Social Justice Research, 17*(2), 111–115.

Dalton, J. C., & Crosby, P. C. (2010). College peer culture: Taming the "monster within the gates". *Journal of College and Character, 11*(4), 1–8. doi:10.2202/1940-1639.1749

Feldman, K. A., & Newcomb, T. M. (1969). *The impact of college on students.* San Francisco, CA: Jossey-Bass.

Howe, N., & Strauss, W. (2000). *Millennials rising: The next great generation.* New York, NY: Random House.

Milem, J. F. (1998). Examining the effect of college peer groups and faculty normative groups. *Journal of Higher Education, 69*(2), 117–140.

Moffat, M. (1989). *Coming of age in New Jersey: College and American culture.* New Brunswick, NJ: Rutgers University Press.

Parks, S. (2000). *Big questions, worthy dreams. Mentoring emerging adults in their search for meaning, purpose and faith.* San Francisco, CA: John Wiley & Sons.

Smith, C., Christoffersen, K., Davidson, H., & Herzog, P. S. (2011). *Lost in transition. The dark side of emerging adulthood.* New York, NY: Oxford University Press, Inc.

JON C. DALTON *is an emeritus professor of higher education at Florida State University. He is coeditor of the NASPA* Journal of College and Character *and former vice president for student affairs at Florida State University.*

This chapter reviews the different theoretical perspectives and measurements of ethics-related leadership models, including ethical leadership, transformational leadership, authentic leadership, servant leadership, spiritual leadership, and a virtues-based approach to leadership ethics. The similarities and differences among these theoretical models and measures to ethics-related leadership are discussed.

A Critical Review of Theories and Measures of Ethics-Related Leadership

Weichun Zhu, Xiaoming Zheng, Ronald E. Riggio, Xi Zhang

In recent years, publicized business leadership scandals, recent collapses of a number of financial institutions, and broad societal challenges facing both public and private organizations have called for urgent attention to leadership ethics (Trevino, den Nieuwenboer, & Kish-Gephart, 2014). As a result, researchers in management and other related fields are becoming increasingly interested in the ethics of leadership, including investigating different theories, structures and means of measuring ethics-related leadership.

In this chapter, we conduct a comprehensive review of ethics-related leadership models. Our review focuses not only on the similarities and differences of these definitions and models but also on their scales of ethics-related leadership. Based on the review, we also discuss the importance and strengths of using a virtue approach to measure leadership ethics and one virtue-based leadership ethics scale, in particular, called the Leadership Virtues Questionnaire (LVQ; Riggio, Zhu, Reina, & Maroosis, 2010).

Overview of Ethical Leadership

Many researchers have linked ethical leadership with individual ethical characteristics and leaders' moral conduct (Bass & Steidlmeier, 1999; Kacmar, Bachrach, Harris, & Zivnuska, 2011). For example, when a leader's actions are consistent with his or her beliefs and ethical standards, then he or she would be regarded as an ethical leader, or when he or she is motivated by altruism rather than selfishness, he or she would also be considered an

NEW DIRECTIONS FOR STUDENT LEADERSHIP, no. 146, Summer 2015 © 2015 Wiley Periodicals, Inc., A Wiley Company
Published online in Wiley Online Library (wileyonlinelibrary.com) • DOI: 10.1002/yd.20137

ethical leader (Mayer, Aquino, Greenbaum, & Kuenzi, 2012). Ethical leaders should share ethics and values with followers, make tough decisions based on high standards of ethical conduct, inspire followers to implement a vision, and aspire to build a community based on social justice (Brown & Trevino, 2006).

Trevino and her colleagues (Brown & Trevino, 2006; Trevino, Hartman, & Brown, 2000) assert that ethical leadership includes two components, the "moral person" and the "moral manager." To be a moral person, ethical leaders are supposed to possess some personal characteristics and traits, such as honesty, integrity, and trustworthiness. In addition, ethical leaders are also objective and fair decision makers, hold a solid set of ethical values and principles, show extensive social concerns about the society and community, and commit to their ethical decision rules. Ethical leaders are also committed to certain kinds of moral behaviors, such as "doing the right thing, showing concern for people and treating people right, being open and communicative, and demonstrating morality in one's personal life" (Trevino et al., 2000, pp. 131–132).

To be a moral manager, ethical leaders serve as a role model for ethical conduct visibly and intentionally to influence their followers' ethical decision making processes and actions. These ethical managers communicate regularly their ethical values, standards, and principles to their followers and aspire to establish reward and punishment systems that consistently hold all followers accountable for ethical conduct (Schaubreck et al., 2012; Trevino et al., 2000).

Furthermore, Trevino and her colleagues defined ethical leadership as "the demonstration of normatively appropriate conduct through personal actions and interpersonal relationships, and the promotion of such conduct to followers through two-way communication, reinforcement, and decision-making" (Brown, Trevino, & Harrison, 2005, p. 120). The first part of this definition means that by demonstrating normatively appropriate personal traits and behaviors, leaders embody the "moral person" dimension.

The second part of the definition means that ethical leaders try to make ethical standards, values, and principles salient by communicating regularly to followers, and through this two-way process, followers are able to emulate their leaders' ethical behaviors spontaneously and eventually identify with them. Beyond that, ethical leaders reward ethical conduct and punish unethical conduct holding all followers accountable for engaging in ethical decision making. This component is more consistent with the "moral manager" dimension.

The Ethical Leadership Scale (ELS).   Based on the above conceptualization, Brown et al. (2005) took a descriptive perspective to develop a ten-item instrument, called the Ethical Leadership Scale (ELS), to measure ethical leadership. They conducted a series of studies to investigate the discriminative, nomological and predictive validity of this scale. It was found that the ELS was positively associated with leader consideration behaviors, interactional fairness, leader honesty, the idealized influence dimension of transformational leadership and negatively related to abusive supervision. Furthermore, the ethical leadership scale predicted followers' satisfaction with the leader, affective trust in the leader, job dedication, leader effectiveness and followers' willingness to report problems to management (Brown et al., 2005). The ELS has been used extensively in the empirical research (e.g., Mayer et al., 2012; Schaubreck et al., 2012).

There are several notes that need to be made regarding the ELS. First, there are some key differences regarding the dimensions of ethical leadership between the qualitative interview results of Trevino et al. (2000) and those measured in the ELS by Brown et al. (2005). More specifically, according to Trevino et al. (2000), the ethical leadership construct is comprised of two dimensions: "moral person" and "moral manager." Interestingly, in the ELS scale, these two aspects collapse into a single dimension. Though the 10 items of ELS have more or less covered the "moral person" and "moral manager" aspects, some important traits associated with ethics, such as integrity and honesty, are omitted. It is doubtful that the broad domain of ethical leadership can be fully covered with this 10-item scale. As pointed out by Kalshoven, Den Hartog, and De Hoogh (2011), theoretically speaking, the underlying ethical leadership behaviors are rather different and might have different antecedents and consequences. Therefore, combining such diverse and different behaviors and traits into a single general factor makes it harder to explore the specific effects of a certain component of ethical leadership, let alone its more complex underlying influence mechanisms of ethical leadership on individuals, groups, and companies.

Consequently, through a deductive and inductive approach, Kalshoven et al. (2011) developed a scale, called the Ethical Leadership at Work questionnaire (ELW), to measure different forms of ethical leadership behaviors. This new scale is a multidimensional one which includes these seven components: fairness, integrity, ethical guidance, people orientation, power sharing, role clarification, and concern for sustainability. The ELW scale is positively related to transformational leadership, transactional leadership, the ELS, and negatively related to autocratic and passive leadership. Also, the ELW predicted a series of followers' work attitudes, such as perceived leader effectiveness, trust in management, job and leader satisfaction, and organizational commitment.

The ELW is a multidimensional scale, but most of the items are aimed at measuring the "moral manager" dimensions. Few items measure the "moral person" dimension. For example, items, such as "take time to talk about work-related emotions (people orientation)," "delegates challenging responsibilities to subordinates (power sharing)," "shows concern for sustainability issues (concern for sustainability)" and "clearly explains integrity related codes of conduct," all measure manager behaviors. Only some items such as "keeps his or her promises" and "can be trusted to do the things he or she says" are related to personal traits or characteristics.

The item generation process is a combination of a qualitative interview and literature review. However, the theoretical framework used to develop the seven ethical behaviors is derived from different literatures and seems to lack a solid theoretical foundation. Furthermore, some dimensions, such as role clarification, appear to be more like neutral leadership behaviors rather than ethics-related behaviors. Another limitation for the ELW is its predictive validity. So far, none of the outcomes (organizational citizenship behavior, trust in management, job satisfaction) used in the Kalshoven et al. (2011) study is concerned with followers' ethical behaviors. As a result, the predictive validity of the scale to affect followers' ethics-related behaviors still needs further investigation. As the authors suggest, employees' ethics-related variables, such as moral identity, should be considered in future research.

Overview of Transformational Leadership

The second ethics-related leadership approach we will discuss is transformational leadership, which is defined as:

> Those who stimulate and inspire followers to both achieve extraordinary outcomes and, in the process, develop their own leadership capacity. Transformational leaders help followers grow and develop into leaders by responding to individual followers' needs by empowering them and by aligning the objectives and goals of the individual followers, the leader, the group, and the larger organization. (Bass & Riggio, 2006, p. 3)

Burns (1978) asserted that transforming leaders had to be morally uplifting. It was ethics that distinguished truly transformational leaders from pseudo-transformational leaders (Bass & Steidlmeier, 1999). Burns (1978) originally proposed that transformational leadership was moral leadership, because such leaders inspired followers by aligning their own and their followers' value systems toward important moral principles. But Bass (1985), who provided the means to measure transforming/transformational leadership, initially expected the dynamics of transformational leadership to be the same whether the leader was beneficial or harmful to others.

Through a lot of debate and discussion, Bass and Steidlmeier (1999) agreed that transformational leaders could be unethical, and transformational leadership and ethical leadership were not necessarily aligned, which is also acclaimed by Brown et al. (2005). As a result, they distinguished authentic transformational leaders (ethical leaders) from pseudo-transformational leaders (unethical leaders). Authentic transformational leaders are moral leaders, because they transcend their own self-interests and focus more on the greater good based on moral principles. They do the right thing, what fits the principles of morality, responsibility, sense of discipline and respect for authority, customs, rules, and traditions of a society (Bass & Riggio, 2006). In contrast, pseudo-transformational leaders are self-concerned, exploitative, and power oriented. They believe in warped moral principles. So we see that ethics are a critical element for truly transformational leadership. In recent years, scholars have begun to examine the relationship between transformational leadership and ethical leadership behavior (Brown et al., 2005; Zhu, Avolio, Riggio, & Sosik, 2011).

Multifactor Leadership Questionnaire (MLQ). The Multifactor Leadership Questionnaire (MLQ), developed by Bass and Avolio (1997), is the most commonly used leadership scale. The current, revised form of the MLQ (Bass & Avolio, 1997) contains 36 standardized items, with four items assessing each of the nine leadership dimensions associated with the Full Range of Leadership model. 20 items are used to measure five dimensions of transformational leadership: inspirational motivation, idealized influence (attributes and behaviors), individualized consideration, and intellectual stimulation.

Of these, the idealized influence dimension is explicitly defined as having an ethics component. Eight items are used to measure idealized influence, termed as "idealized influence attributes (IIA)" and "idealized influence behaviors (IIB)." Sample items of idealized influence attributes are "goes beyond self-interest" and "displays power and confidence." Sample items for idealized influence behaviors (IIB) include "considers the moral or ethical consequences of their decisions" and "emphasizes the collective mission." Transformational leadership and ethical leadership overlap in certain aspects, because both constructs are concerned about others, act consistently in line with their moral principles, consider the ethical consequences of their decisions, "can be counted on to do the right thing," and display "high standards of ethical and moral conduct" (Avolio, 1999). One fact to note, however, is that the MLQ has only one item that directly measures the ethics of the leader. This item is "the leader considers the moral consequence of his/her decision" (Bass & Avolio, 1997). The broad domain of ethics of leadership is unlikely to be covered with only one item.

Overview of Authentic Leadership

Gardner, Avolio, and Walumbwa (2005) proposed a self-based model of authentic leader and follower development which focuses on the core self-awareness and self-regulation components of authentic leadership. They identified several distinguishing features associated with authentic self-regulation processes, including internalized regulation, balanced information processing, relational transparency, and authentic behavior.

Building on the previous work, Walumbwa, Avolio, Gardner, Wernsing, and Peterson (2008) provided a refined definition of authentic leadership that more fully reflects the underlying dimensions of the construct posited by Gardner et al. (2005). They define authentic leadership as

> a pattern of leader behavior that draws upon and promotes both positive psychological capacities and a positive ethical climate, to foster greater self-awareness, an internalized moral perspective, balanced processing of information, and relational transparency on the part of leaders working with followers, fostering positive self-development. (Walumbwa et al., 2008, p. 94)

Of the four dimensions, "internalized moral perspective" was given enough attention and put in the central role, which suggests that even if under group, organizational, and societal pressures, authentic leaders would keep their behaviors and decision making guided by their internal moral standards and values (Gardner et al., 2005).

Authentic Leadership Scale (ALS).   Based on the above definition, Walumbwa et al. (2008) used deductive and inductive methods to develop an instrument to measure authentic leadership. Confirmatory factor analyses results supported a higher order, multidimensional model of the authentic leadership construct. The Authentic Leadership Scale (ALS) comprises 16 items in total. Of these, four items are used to measure self-awareness, five items measure relational transparency, four items measure internalized moral perspective, and three items are used to measure balanced processing.

Two sample items of "internalized moral perspective" are "makes decisions based on his or her core values" and "makes difficult decisions based on high standards of ethical conduct." It is suggested that authentic leaders present a positive moral perspective characterized by high ethical standards, values, and the considering of ethical consequences of their decisions. Though four items of the internalized moral perspective assess the moral aspect of leadership, they are too narrow to capture the whole domain of ethical leadership. Although they partially focus on the "moral person" aspect of ethical leadership, the "moral manager" dimension is not adequately measured with these items.

Overview of Servant Leadership

Greenleaf's (1977) seminal work served as a starting point for the theory of servant leadership. Greenleaf (1977) described the leader as a servant first:

> It begins with the natural feeling that one wants to serve, to serve first. Then conscious choice brings one to aspire to lead. That person is sharply different from one who is leader first . . . The difference manifests itself in the care taken by the servant—first to make sure that other people's highest priority needs are being served. The best test is: Do those served grow as persons; do they, while being served, become healthier, wiser, freer, more autonomous, more likely themselves to become servants? (Greenleaf, 1977, p. 27)

Spears (1998) extended Greenleaf's work and concluded that Greenleaf's (1977) writings incorporated 10 major attributes of servant leadership. They were listening, empathy, healing, awareness, persuasion, conceptualization, foresight, stewardship, commitment to the growth of people, and building community. This provided the closest representation of an articulated framework for what characterizes servant leadership.

Based on the earlier conceptual work (Greenleaf, 1977; Spears, 1998), Russell and Stone (2002) further developed servant leadership theory. They divided 20 attributes of servant leadership into two broad categories. The first category of functional attributes include vision, honesty, integrity, trust, service, modeling, pioneering, appreciation of others, and empowerment. These attributes are the operative qualities, characteristics, and distinctive features that are associated with a servant leader. The second category of servant leadership attributes, called "accompanying attributes," include communication, credibility, competence, stewardship, visibility, influence, persuasion, listening, encouragement, teaching, and delegation, which are more behavioral items. We must note that this type of classification is a theoretical and descriptive discussion of servant leadership, not an empirical one. In this conceptual model, some of the personal traits, such as honesty, integrity, and creditability, are associated with the "moral person" dimension of ethical leadership, while behavioral items such as modeling and pioneering overlap with the "moral manager" dimension of ethical leadership.

Scales of Servant Leadership. Several researchers have developed scales to measure servant leadership. Barbuto and Wheeler (2006) combined the 10 characteristics of Spears (1998) with a dimension called "the natural desire to serve others," which was fundamental to servant leadership in the early writings of Greenleaf (1977). These researchers developed operational definitions and scales to measure 11 potential characteristics of servant leadership. Factor analyses reduced this scale to five unique dimensions: altruistic calling (four items), emotional healing (four items), wisdom (five items), persuasive mapping (five items), and organizational stewardship (five items). Among these five dimensions, altruistic calling is most aligned with ethics.

Another group of researchers, Liden, Wayne, Zhao, and Henderson (2008) developed a seven-dimension scale to measure servant leadership. These seven dimensions are conceptual skills, empowering, helping subordinates grow and succeed, putting subordinates first, behaving ethically, emotional healing, and creating value for the community. Each dimension is assessed by four items, totaling 28 items for this scale.

In the Liden et al.'s (2008) scale, the "behaving ethically" dimension contains four items directly assessing ethics. These items include "my manager holds high ethical standards," "my manager is always honest," "my manager would not compromise ethical principles in order to achieve success," and "my manager values honesty more than profits." These four items are more like the "moral person" dimension of ethical leadership, although these items do not necessarily cover the entire broad domain of ethical leadership.

Overview of Spiritual Leadership

Fry (2003) first defined spiritual leadership as "comprising the values, attitudes, and behaviors that are necessary to intrinsically motivate one's self and others so that they have a sense of spiritual survival through calling and membership" (pp. 694–695). He also explained that two elements are necessary for spiritual leadership. Leaders need to create a vision, so that followers are able to experience a sense of meaning for, and impact of, their lives. Spiritual leaders should develop an organizational culture that is based on altruistic love whereby leaders and followers could develop genuine caring, concern, and appreciation for each other (Fry, 2003).

Spiritual leaders create a clear and compelling vision for their followers and rely on hope and faith, which can cultivate followers' beliefs, conviction, trust, and actions to work toward achieving the vision. Spiritual leadership motivates followers to act intrinsically and to produce a sense of calling—making a difference through service to others and deriving meaning and purpose in life (Pfeffer, 2003). Furthermore, organizations also show altruistic love to their organizational members who will be motivated to internalize a common vision and to establish a sense of membership within organizations.

Spiritual Leadership Questionnaire. Fry, Vitucci, and Credillo (2005) developed a five-dimensional instrument to measure spiritual leadership. These five dimensions are vision, hope/faith, altruistic love, meaning, and membership. Among these five dimensions, altruistic love, defined as "a sense of wholeness, harmony, and well-being produced through care, concern, and appreciation for both self and others" (Fry et al., 2005, p. 844), is similar to the "moral person" dimension of ethical leadership. There are seven items used to measure altruistic love. Sample items include "the leaders in my organization are honest and without false pride" and "the leaders in my organization have the courage to stand up for their people." This dimension is also consistent with the virtue perspective of Riggio et al. (2010) which will be discussed shortly. Although this scale of spiritual leadership has covered some characteristics of ethical leadership, it does not capture the whole domain of the "moral person" and "moral manager."

Overview of Leadership Virtues

Several of these approaches to leadership ethics include explicit or implicit references to virtues (e.g., authentic leadership, spiritual leadership).

A recent theoretical perspective is based on the ancient philosophical approach of Aristotle and an emphasis on the cardinal virtues as a means of conceptualizing and assessing ethical leadership (Riggio et al., 2010). This virtues approach defines the ethical leader as "a leader whose personal characteristics and actions align with each of the four cardinal virtues of prudence, temperance, fortitude, and justice" (Riggio et al., 2010, p. 239).

The first cardinal virtue is *prudence*, and it is often associated with knowledge, practical wisdom and insight. According to Aristotle (350 BCE/2005), prudence is used to describe the ability to find the balance between two extremes and make the appropriate decision that both minimizes harm and maximizes the good.

The second cardinal virtue is *fortitude* (often called courage). This means that courageous leaders will act prudently and "stand immovable in the midst of dangers" (Thomas Aquinas, 1265–1274/2005, p.109). With fortitude, leaders can possess the mind and spirit that enables them to face up to ethical challenges firmly and confidently (Thomas Aquinas, 1265–1274/2005).

Temperance is the ability to control one's emotions. The idea of moderation is critical to the understanding of temperance. Temperate leaders know how to control their bodies and their physical needs and do not practice acts of self-indulgence or self-denial. A temperate person avoids being overly occupied with an intense desire to pursue physical pleasure and shows a restrained (and prudent) desire of physical gratification.

The fourth cardinal virtue, *justice*, was given great attention by Aristotle. He talks about two distinct types of justice: *general justice* that deals mostly with following laws (something is unjust if it is unlawful); and *particular justice* which deals with fairness (something is unjust if it is not fair; Aristotle, 350 BCE/2005). Aristotle (350 BCE/2005) describes an unjust action as one that is motivated by unjust gains. Justice is a sustained or constant willingness to give others what they deserve (e.g., basic human rights; Aquinas, 1265–1274/2005, p. 35).

The Leadership Virtues Questionnaire (LVQ).   Based on the above definitions, Riggio et al. (2010) developed a 19-item scale, called the Leadership Virtues Questionnaire (LVQ), to measure the construct of virtue-based ethical leadership. Of these, five items are used to measure prudence, five items measure fortitude, six items assess justice, and three items measure temperance. A series of studies has established the initial reliability and validity of this scale.

The LVQ is found to be highly positively correlated with transformational leadership, authentic leadership, and the ELS. Most importantly, followers with more virtuous leaders feel a stronger sense of personal moral identity, feel more empowered by their leaders, and demonstrate greater organizational identification than those with less virtuous leaders (Riggio et al., 2010).

Discussion

Although all of the theories and measurement scales discussed here are related to leadership ethics in some ways, none of these instruments of ethical leadership, transformational leadership, authentic leadership, servant leadership, spiritual leadership, and virtuous leadership are able to fully cover the domain of ethical leadership, as represented by Trevino et al. (2000), in their discussion of the "moral person" and the "moral manager." Table 7.1 compares and contrasts the various theories and scales using the Trevino et al. (2000) conceptual framework. As shown in Table 7.1, another limitation is that most of these researchers relied more on the descriptive approach rather than using a robust theoretical perspective to develop the scales to measure leadership ethics.

It is important to note that with the exception of transformational leadership theory and the MLQ, all of these theories and measures have been published in the past 6 years, and some are "hot off the press." It is only very recently that management theorists and psychologists interested in leadership have begun to seriously study leadership ethics, and there are some problems remaining.

First, there is a great deal of overlap between these various theoretical models, and research with the various scales is still in the early stages. However, one troubling finding is that the various measures are all highly intercorrelated. In fact, Riggio et al. (2010) note that the relationships

Table 7.1   Comparing Various Ethics-Related Leadership Scales
Using the Trevino et al. (2003) Two Dimensions

			ELS	ELW	MLQ	ALQ	SLQ	SPLQ	LVQ
Moral person	Traits	Integrity	√	√					√
		Honesty	√			√	√		√
		Trustworthiness	√					√	√
	Behaviors	Do the right thing	√						√
		Concern for people	√	√			√	√	√
		Being open	√	√					√
		Personal morality	√						√
	Decision-making	Hold to values			√	√			
		Objective	√		√				√
		Concern for society	√	√					
		Follow ethical decision rules	√			√			
Moral manager	Role modeling through visible action		√						
	Rewards and discipline		√						
	Communicating ethics and values		√	√					

Note: ELS = Ethical Leadership Scale; ELW = Ethical Leadership at Work; MLQ = Multifactor Leadership Questionnaire; ALQ = Authentic Leadership Questionnaire; SLQ = Servant Leadership Questionnaire; SPLQ = Spiritual Leadership Questionnaire; LVQ = Leadership Virtues Questionnaire.

among measures hailing from different theoretical perspectives, such as transformational leadership, ethical leadership, and virtuous leadership, correlate *too highly*—suggesting that they may be indistinguishable psychometrically. The problem may be that they all use the same methodology of having others (usually followers of leaders) rate the leaders' ethics/authenticity/spirituality/virtues. It is likely that followers do not make fine distinctions about the ethical qualities and behaviors of their leaders: rather they make a holistic, summary judgment of whether the leader is or is not a "good" person.

Another issue involves the depth of research on leader ethics. Although these various instruments assess perceptions of leader ethics or character, they have not, except in the most rudimentary fashion, been correlated with the ethicality of a leader's real actions, particularly over a long span of time. For example, some leaders who are perceived to be ethical by those around them in their groups or organizations may display public ethical behavior but engage in unethical acts in private. We also do not know about the stability of ethical leader behavior. For instance, are ethical leaders persons of high character who are consistently ethical in their behavior over time, or can some become "fallen angels" susceptible to temptation? It would seem that issues such as these might differentiate more character-based approaches to leader ethics from the more behaviorally-based theoretical approaches.

Conclusion

We began by reviewing the recent social-scientific literature regarding ethics-related leadership and its measurement. We compared the similarities and differences among various ethics-related leadership theories and measures. These scales adopt fairly different theoretical perspective and research methods and have provided scholars and practitioners an appreciation for the complexity and dynamics of ethics-related leadership. However, because ethics-related leadership research is a rather new paradigm in the field of management/organizational psychology, more rigorous theory-based social-scientific approaches to ethics-related leadership are definitely needed to help researchers further understand this important topic. As reviewed above, the construct and measurement developments of ethics-related leadership have, in a very short space of time, begun to make progress in providing more options for assessing ethics-related leadership. It is hoped that this review of theories and measures will stimulate additional research efforts from scholars in the field.

References

Aquinas, T. (2005). *The cardinal virtues: Prudence, justice, fortitude, and temperance* (R. J. Regan, Trans.). Indianapolis, IN: Hackett Publishing. (Original work written 1265–1274)

Aristotle. (2005). *Nicomachean ethics*. (W. D. Ross, Trans.). Cambridge: Cambridge University Press. (Original work published 350 BCE).

Avolio, B. J. (1999). *Full leadership development: Building the vital forces in organizations*. Newbury Park, CA: Sage.

Barbuto, J. E., Jr., & Wheeler, D. W. (2006). Scale development and construct clarification of servant leadership. *Group and Organization Management, 31*, 300–326.

Bass, B. M. (1985). *Leadership and performance beyond expectations*. New York, NY: Free Press.

Bass, B. M., & Avolio, B. J. (1997). *Revised manual for the multifactor leadership questionnaire*. Palo Alto, CA: Mind Garden.

Bass, B. M., & Riggio, R. E. (2006). *Transformational leadership*. Mahwah, NJ: Lawrence Erlbaum Associates.

Bass, B. M., & Steidlmeier, P. (1999). Ethics, character, and authentic transformational leadership behavior. *Leadership Quarterly, 10*, 181–217.

Brown, M. E., & Trevino, L. K. (2006). Ethical leadership: A review and future directions. *The Leadership Quarterly, 17*, 595–616.

Brown, M. E., Trevino, L. K., & Harrison, D. (2005). Ethical leadership: A social learning perspective for construct development and testing. *Organizational Behavior and Human Decision Processes, 97*, 117–134.

Burns, J. M. (1978). *Leadership*. New York, NY: Harper & Row.

Fry, L. W. (2003). Toward a theory of spiritual leadership. *The Leadership Quarterly, 14*, 693–727.

Fry, L. W., Vitucci, S., & Cedillo, M. (2005). Spiritual leadership and army transformation: Theory, measurement, and establishing a baseline. *The Leadership Quarterly, 16*, 835–862.

Gardner, W. L., Avolio, B. J., & Walumbwa, F. O. (2005). Authentic leadership development: Emergent trends and future directions. In W. L. Gardner, B. J. Avolio, & F. O. Walumbwa (Eds.), *Authentic leadership theory and practice: Origins, effects and development* (pp. 387–406). Oxford, UK: Elsevier Science.

Greenleaf, R. K. (1977). *Servant leadership: A journey into the nature of legitimate power and greatness*. Mahwah, NJ: Paulist Press.

Kacmar, K. M., Bachrach, D. G., Harris, K. J., & Zivnuska, S. (2011). Fostering good citizenship through ethical leadership: Exploring the moderating role of gender and organizational politics. *Journal of Applied Psychology, 96*(3), 633–642.

Kalshoven, K., Den Hartog, D. N., & De Hoogh, A. H. B. (2011). Ethical leadership at work questionnaire (ELW): Development and validation of a multidimensional measure. *The Leadership Quarterly, 22*, 51–69.

Liden, R. C., Wayne, S. J., Zhao, H., & Henderson, D. (2008). Servant leadership: Development of a multidimensional measure and multi-level assessment. *The Leadership Quarterly, 19*, 161–177.

Mayer, D. M., Aquino, K., Greenbaum, R. L., & Kuenzi, M. (2012). Who displays ethical leadership, and why does it matter? An examination of antecedents and consequences of ethical leadership. *Academy of Management Journal, 55*(1), 151–171.

Pfeffer, J. (2003). Business and the spirit. In R. A. Giacalone & C. L. Jurkiewicz (Eds.), *Handbook of workplace spirituality and organizational performance* (pp. 29–45). New York, NY: M. E. Sharp.

Riggio, R. E., Zhu, W., Reina, C., & Maroosis, J. A. (2010). Virtue-based measurement of ethical leadership: The Leadership Virtues Questionnaire. *Consulting Psychology Journal: Practice and Research, 62*, 235–250.

Russell, R. F., & Stone, A. G. (2002). A review of servant leadership attributes: Developing a practical model. *Leadership and Organization Development Journal, 23*, 145–157.

Schaubreck, J. M., Hannah, S. T., Avolio, B. J., Kozlowski, S. W., Lord, R. G., Trevino, L. K., . . . et al. (2012). Embedding ethical leadership within and across organizational levels. *Academy of Management Journal, 55*(5), 1053–1078.

Spears, L. C. (1998). Tracing the growing impact of servant leadership. In L. C. Spears (Ed.), *Insights on leadership: Service, stewardship, spirit, and servant-leadership* (pp. 1–12). New York, NY: John Wiley & Sons.

Trevino, L. K., den Nieuwenboer, N. A., & Kish-Gephart, J. J. (2014). (Un)ethical behavior in organizations. *Annual Review of Psychology, 65*, 635–660.

Trevino, L. K., Hartman, L. P., & Brown, M. (2000). Moral person and moral manager: How executives develop a reputation for ethical leadership. *California Management Review, 42*, 128–142.

Walumbwa, F. O., Avolio, B. J., Gardner, W. L., Wernsing, T. S., & Peterson, S. J. (2008). Authentic leadership: Development and validation of a theory-based measure. *Journal of Management, 34*, 89–126.

Zhu, W., Avolio, B. J., Riggio, R., & Sosik, J. (2011). The effect of authentic transformational leadership on follower and group ethics. *The Leadership Quarterly, 22*, 801–817.

WEICHUN ZHU *is an assistant professor at the School of Labor and Employment Relations at Pennsylvania State University.*

XIAOMING ZHENG *is an associate professor of leadership and organization management in the School of Economics and Management at Tsinghua University of China.*

RONALD E. RIGGIO *is the Henry R. Kravis Professor of Leadership and Organizational Psychology at Claremont McKenna College.*

XI ZHANG *is a human resource specialist at Sinochem Petroleum Exploration and Production Co., Ltd. in Beijing, China.*

Appendix: Sample Items for Each Scale

Ethical Leadership Scale

Conducts his/her personal life in an ethical manner

Listens to what employees have to say

Source: Brown, M. E., Trevino, L. K., & Harrison, D. (2005). Ethical leadership: A social learning perspective for construct development and testing. *Organizational Behavior and Human Decision Processes, 97,* 117–134.

Ethical Leadership at Work (ELW)

People orientation

Is interested in how I feel and how I am doing.

Is genuinely concerned about my personal development.

Fairness

Holds me responsible for things that are not my fault. (R)

Pursues his/her own success at the expense of others. (R)

Power sharing

Allows subordinates to influence critical decisions.

Permits me to play a key role in setting my own performance goals.

Concern for sustainability

Would like to work in an environmentally friendly manner.

Shows concern for sustainability issues.

Ethical guidance

Clearly explains integrity related codes of conduct.

Explains what is expected from employees in terms of behaving with integrity.

Role clarification

Indicates what the performance expectations of each group member are.

Explains what is expected of each group member.

Integrity

Keeps his/her promises.

Can be trusted to do the things he/she says.

Source: Kalshoven, K., Den Hartog, D.N., & De Hoogh, A. H. B. (2011). Ethical leadership at work questionnaire (ELW): Development and validation of a multidimensional measure. *The Leadership Quarterly, 22,* 51–69.

Transformational Leadership (MLQ)

Go beyond self-interest for the good of the group

Consider the moral and ethical consequences of decisions

Source: Avolio, B. J., Bass, B., Walumbwa, F. O., & Zhu, W. (2004). *MLQ Multifactor Leadership Questionnaire* (3rd ed.). Redwood, CA: Mind Garden.

Authentic Leadership Scale

Says exactly what he/she means.

Demonstrates beliefs that are consistent with actions.

Solicits views that challenge his/her deeply held positions.

Seeks feedback to improve interactions with others.

Source: Walumbwa, F. O., Avolio, B. J., Gardner, W. L., Wernsing, T. S., & Peterson, S. J. (2008). Authentic leadership: Development and validation of a theory-based measure. *Journal of Management, 34,* 89–126

Servant Leadership Scale (1)

I would seek help from my manager if I had a personal problem.

My manager emphasizes the importance of giving back to the community.

My manager is able to effectively think through complex problems.

My manager gives me the responsibility to make important decisions about my job.

My manager makes my career development a priority.

My manager provides me with work experiences that enable me to develop new skills.

My manager puts my best interests ahead of his/her own.

My manager holds high ethical standards.

My manager is always honest.

Source: Liden, R. C., Wayne, S. J., Zhao, H., & Henderson, D. (2008). Servant leadership: Development of a multidimensional measure and multilevel assessment. *The Leadership Quarterly, 19,* 161–177.

Servant Leadership Scale (2)

Altruistic calling

This person puts my best interests ahead of his/her own.

This person does everything he/she can to serve me.

Emotional healing

This person is one I would turn to if I had a personal trauma.

This person is good at helping me with my emotional issues.

Wisdom

This person seems alert to what's happening.

This person is good at anticipating the consequences of decisions.

Persuasive mapping

This person offers compelling reasons to get me to do things.

This person encourages me to dream "big dreams" about the organization.

Organizational stewardship

This person believes that the organization needs to play a moral role in society.

This person believes that our organization needs to function as a community.

Source: Barbuto, J. E., Jr., & Wheeler, D. W. (2006). Scale development and construct clarification of servant leadership. *Group and Organization Management, 31,* 300–326.

Spiritual Leadership Scale

Vision—describes the organization's journey and why we are taking it; defines who we are and what we do.

I understand and am committed to my organization's vision.

My workgroup has a vision statement that brings out the best in me.

Hope/faith—the assurance of things hoped for, the conviction that the organization's vision/purpose/mission will be fulfilled.

I have faith in my organization and I am willing to do whatever it takes to insure that it accomplishes its mission.

I persevere and exert extra effort to help my organization succeed because I have faith in what it stands for.

Altruistic love—a sense of wholeness, harmony, and well-being produced through care, concern, and appreciation for both self and others.

The leaders in my organization walk the walk as well as talk the talk.

The leaders in my organization are honest and without false pride.

Source: Fry, L. W., Vitucci, S., & Cedillo, M. (2005). Spiritual leadership and army transformation: Theory, measurement, and establishing a baseline. *The Leadership Quarterly, 16,* 835–862.

The Leadership Virtue Questionnaire

Prudence

Does as he/she ought to do in a given situation.

Does not carefully consider all the information available before making an important decision that impacts others. (R)

Fortitude

Would rather risk his/her job than do something that was unjust.

May have difficulty standing up for his/her beliefs among friends who do not share the same views. (R)

Temperance

Seems to be overly concerned with his/her personal power. (R)

Is not overly concerned with his/her own accomplishments.

Justice

Gives credit to others when credit is due.

Demonstrates respect for all people.

Source: Riggio, R. E., Zhu, W., Reina, C., & Maroosis, J. A. (2010). Virtue-based measurement of ethical leadership: The Leadership Virtues Questionnaire. *Consulting Psychology Journal: Practice and Research, 62,* 235–250.

Index

NEW DIRECTIONS FOR STUDENT LEADERSHIP
ORDER FORM SUBSCRIPTION AND SINGLE ISSUES

DISCOUNTED BACK ISSUES:

Use this form to receive 20% off all back issues of *New Directions for Student Leadership*.
All single issues priced at **$23.20** (normally $29.00)

TITLE	ISSUE NO.	ISBN

Call 1-800-835-6770 or see mailing instructions below. When calling, mention the promotional code JBNND to receive your discount.

SUBSCRIPTIONS: (1 YEAR, 4 ISSUES)

☐ New Order   ☐ Renewal

U.S.	☐ Individual: $89	☐ Institutional: $342
CANADA/MEXICO	☐ Individual: $89	☐ Institutional: $382
ALL OTHERS	☐ Individual: $113	☐ Institutional: $416

Call 1-800-835-6770 or see mailing and pricing instructions below.
Online subscriptions are available at www.onlinelibrary.wiley.com

ORDER TOTALS:

Issue / Subscription Amount: $ _____

Shipping Amount: $ _____
(for single issues only – subscription prices include shipping)

Total Amount: $ _____

SHIPPING CHARGES:	
First Item	$6.00
Each Add'l Item	$2.00

(No sales tax for U.S. subscriptions. Canadian residents, add GST for subscription orders. Individual rate subscriptions must be paid by personal check or credit card. Individual rate subscriptions may not be resold as library copies.)

BILLING & SHIPPING INFORMATION:

☐ **PAYMENT ENCLOSED:** *(U.S. check or money order only. All payments must be in U.S. dollars.)*

☐ **CREDIT CARD:**   ☐ VISA   ☐ MC   ☐ AMEX

Card number _____ Exp. Date _____

Card Holder Name _____ Card Issue # _____

Signature _____ Day Phone _____

☐ **BILL ME:** *(U.S. institutional orders only. Purchase order required.)*

Purchase order # _____
    Federal Tax ID 13559302 • GST 89102-8052

Name _____

Address _____

Phone _____ E-mail _____

Copy or detach page and send to: **John Wiley & Sons, One Montgomery Street, Suite 1000,**
San Francisco, CA 94104-4594

Order Form can also be faxed to: **888-481-2665**

PROMO JBNND